Preparing to Prepare

A General Guide to

Self-Sufficiency & Preparedness

Preparing to Prepare

*A General Guide to
Self-Sufficiency & Preparedness*

By: David J. Kershner

Table of Contents

Introduction

The purpose of this general guide is to present you with as stable a foundation as possible when it comes to thinking about being prepared for what life and Mother Nature throws at you. That being said, let's get a few things out of the way.

1. My goal is not to make anyone feel foolish or ill prepared.
2. I am not the be-all-end-all for preparedness planning information.
3. My knowledge base, skill level, and life experiences are vastly different from yours.
4. There is always more than one way to do something.

My sole aim with this guide is to direct your attention toward things you may not be aware of, have not foreseen, or that flat out never occurred to you, period. If the information contained herein helps drive and motivate you to begin this journey, try something new, or prompts you to do some additional research on a topic, then I will have been successful.

Many of the topics I am covering can be done in any environment… at least that is what I have tried to do. However, there are some notable exceptions. For example, if you are living in a midtown apartment in Manhattan, you probably don't care about managing your woodlot. However, you might care very much about food, water, and what it means to have more than the FEMA recommended three-day supply of both on hand.

In addition, instead of reinventing the wheel, I'll provide my take on a particular topic and then provide a book recommendation or give you a web address (URL). I am doing this because I am purposefully not writing an anthology for all things preparedness related. All I want to do is give you some useful information that helps you make better decisions. The additional references will help point you in the right direction so that you may further your research into areas and topics that are of interest to you. Please bear in mind that it may prove difficult to embrace some of these concepts if you are subject to burdensome zoning or subject to restrictive rental agreements and Home Owner Associations (HOA).

Chapter 1 - Preparing to Prepare – What Does That Even Mean?

When people hear the words 'self-sufficiency' and 'preparedness' together in the same sentence, they typically conjure up images of a reclusive prepper living off-grid in the woods in a makeshift bunker. While I find this connection hilarious, I also happen to know that those terms get a bad rap. What this guide will show you is that anyone and everyone is, in a general sense, preparing for something. The difference is that we don't ascribe those terms to say:

- Suzy Homemaker who purchased some extra cases of water for her family because the dog days of summer are approaching.
- Johnny Backwater who purchased two dozen sheets of plywood so he could board up his coastal or near-coastal home's windows when the hurricanes start spinning in the Atlantic *(or Bob Bizowner who wanted to protect his business from anarchists, rioters, and looters.)*
- Grandma Betsy who grew and canned produce from the Victory Garden she started seventy-five years ago.
- Uncle Frank who purchased and filled extra cans of gas for his generator so he could keep some appliances running when winter ice arrives and knocks out power.
- Neighbor Jenny who purchased two months' worth of everything (food, water, pet food), N95 masks, bottles of hand-sanitizer, toilet paper, and cleaning supplies just before the panic set in and state lockdowns were initiated during a global pandemic.

When we see examples like these, we say they were smart to be prepared, or had good timing, in a positive way, not derogatorily. The intent of this guide is to highlight specific examples and scenarios and provide real-world solutions and suggestions so you and your family can weather just about anything.

Now, to get things started, let me ask a simple, direct question:

What do you think you need to prepare for?

This is an extremely important question and you *must* ask yourself this. Before you answer it though, I want you to think long and hard about it beforehand. *Do not make a single purchase or decision until you have this answer.*

The reason I say this, and stress it the way I have, is that the answer will *drive* your decision making, thought processes, and spending habits.

Let me ask my question differently and associate it to a duration.

> Are you preparing for a *minor* disruption of services?
> *(1-week max)*

These types of events are generally your weather and natural phenomenon related events. Things like hurricanes, tornadoes, earthquakes, flooding, wildfires, mudslides, ice storms, and blizzards. If this is the case, you are likely to remain in your primary residence, also known as 'sheltering in place'. This assumes that the home isn't uninhabitable.

> Are you preparing for a *moderate* disruption of services?
> *(1-week to 1-month max)*

Again, these typically would encompass your weather and natural phenomenon style events, but of a more extreme variety. Be advised though. There are other items that might fall into both the 'minor' and 'moderate' disruption thought process that are not weather related.

Outside of weather, these disturbances could be, but are definitely not limited to:

- Job loss
- Injury/surgery
- Death in the family
- Long term hospitalization for a family member
- Short/long-term disability

I point to these additional conditions so I can recalibrate your thought processes. You need to think about more than just weather and natural phenomenon. Having noted that, depending on the severity, each of these non-weather related issues could be a major disturbance as well, but I must draw the line somewhere. I have to assume that there are other sources of income (spouse/partner, workers comp, unemployment, insurance settlement, etc.). It is also quite possible that there is potential for additional non-monetary aid from friends, neighbors, churches, relief organizations, the community at large, or even a go-fund me page. That being said, when you are going through it, it will definitely feel like a *major* disruption.

However, *relying* on these sources as your primary source of relief defeats the whole purpose of being self-sufficient.

Are you preparing for a *major* disruption of services?
(4 weeks +)

A major disruption could be anything from long term unemployment, short/long term disability, devastating natural events like a major hurricane, tsunami, solar flare, or earthquake to a national/international financial collapse (Black Swan event), societal collapse, cyber-attack, viral pandemic (SARS, H1N1, COVID-19) or terrorist attack associated with conventional bombings, dirty bombs, electromagnetic pulse (EMPs), etc. Obviously, there are additional scenarios that could be added to the list, but you get the idea. These scale events are generally referred to as SHTF (Shit Hits the Fan) and TEOTWAWKI (The End of the World as We Know It) respectively.

Oh, and while we are here, if the Yellowstone Caldera is your biggest concern, you needn't bother. That is a catastrophic disruptor also referred to as a 'global killer'. The ash cloud, in theory, would wrap our planet like a suffocating blanket and kill all plant life in less than a year. That's assuming you survived the earthquakes that would accompany the explosion. Now assuming you survived all of that, you will most likely be living like a mole... underground. So now, you need to know how to grow food indoors, but you have a bigger problem. Where will you get the water you need for your plants? If there is widespread devastation, you most likely don't have power too because the ash cloud would severely reduce, or more likely eliminate, the efficiency of solar panels. So how are your grow lights going to provide the necessary light for the plants when you can't re-charge your battery banks?

If you actually did try to go outside, the air would be so ash laden that breathing is now a problem without a respirator. Should you decide to trek outside in search of water (after your stored water supply runs out… assuming you stored water for emergencies), despite the potential for respiratory distress, all you're likely to find is that the previously available water sources are now under multiple feet of ash.

Like I said, you needn't bother. It's a global killer.

Now that Yellowstone has been addressed, let me summarize.

The durational length that best defines or suits your needs requires a different level of skill and knowledge and, dare I say, preparedness.

Before we get into defining each of the three duration thresholds, we should discuss some commonsense, everyday pre-disruption planning.

Let's get started.

Chapter 2 - Pre-Disruption Planning – Everyday Needs

With each duration period, there is a certain level of planning that needs to take place. As a result, I have provided a brief run down with regard to planning for each of the durations in Chapter 3-5. That being said, this chapter speaks to preparedness planning in a broad general sense.

In the previous chapter, I asked you if you were thinking about preparing for a minor, moderate, or major disruption. Now that you, hopefully, have an idea as to the duration of what you're planning for, the next question you should ask yourself deals with basic everyday things. *These* answers will ultimately aid you in your immediate short-term emergency planning.

The following subset of questions should get your gears turning as you start thinking about the immediate needs of you and/or your family in the event of a localized issue. Regardless of your living situation (single/divorced, married, widowed, younger/older children, caring for a parent, etc.), you need to have an answer and/or a plan to deal with the following:

1. Do you know what *natural disasters* are prevalent in your area?
2. Do you know if there are any *workplace emergency* plans in place?
3. What are the *school emergency* plans for your kids?
4. What are your community's *evacuation routes*?
5. Where are your *important documents* and information located?
6. What is your current *family emergency plan* including: communications, meeting location, and contact cards?
7. What is the present condition of all of your emergency kits: home, car, evacuation?
8. When was the last time your family sat down and discussed preparedness and emergency response?
9. What is the blood type for each member of the family?

Some of these can be grouped together under a broader heading, but let's look at these nine questions in more detail.

Natural Disasters

The first question, to a certain extent, goes more toward the original question, 'what are you preparing for,' but think hard about this answer. For example, the west coast endured some serious wildfires in 2017 and 2020 where hundreds of thousands of acres burned. In an attempt to curtail some of the origin points, the state's electrical grid was shut down in areas for days at a time. Then, as if that weren't enough, the winter brought torrential rain to the same areas hit by wildfires. Because there was no vegetation left, the rain triggered mudslides that killed dozens and wiped out entire neighborhoods and roadways.

Workplace/School Emergency

Questions two and three are related in the sense that what can happen in a workplace can also happen in a school, that is, depending on the levels of outer security employed at both. For example, school systems and workplaces, by law in most states and jurisdictions, must have an emergency plan on file with a specific State Agency. The question is, do you know what that plan entails? Here's an example of a workplace evacuation plan that was implemented prior to 9/11:

> Of the approximate 2,700 Morgan Stanley staff, only six lives were lost on 9/11 because one man, Rick Rescorla, had the foresight to prepare and orchestrate evacuation drills after the original 1993 bombing at the World Trade Center. With offices located on the 44th through 74th floors of the South Tower, on 9/11, he immediately began moving the staff out of the building when the first plane hit the North Tower, disregarding announcements over the building wide PA system to shelter in place. When the first plane hit, he, and they, knew exactly what to do because they were prepared to evacuate.

Additionally, numerous stories can be found regarding teachers and staff saving student lives during an active shooter situation by either hiding the students, aiding them in escape, or confronting the shooter. Incidentally, police forces are now advising school districts to have their staff escape by any means necessary and to *not* shelter in place during an active shooter situation. Should a student become paralyzed with fear or is injured, they (the teachers and staff) are being instructed to leave them behind.

The examples noted are extreme situations to be sure, but they do need to be planned for accordingly. Most workplace and school emergencies typically deal with power outages, gas/smoke smells, fires, staff health issues, and water main breaks. Regardless, you should know the following:

- What emergency plans does your employer have in place?
- Is there a committee in place to review and update the plans as new information, technology, and situations dictate?
- Do you know where your children will be directed by school administration staff should they be forced to evacuate?
- Is there an alternative pick-up location designated by your school and/or district?
- Have you registered for text, phone, or email messaging in order to receive emergency announcements from your school and/or district?

Evacuation Routes

Knowing designated and alternative evacuation routes is important for several reasons.

1. Stairwells may be blocked, locked, or impassable.
2. Elevators may be automatically disabled by computer control.
3. First responders will immediately close and cordon off street level access to scenes.

Even though question four under 'Everyday Needs' stated 'community' evacuation routes, it is important to think both small and large scale. Knowing how to get out of your building and your community are equally important. The reason being, each of these instances will limit your mobility and your ability to remove yourself from a potentially dangerous situation, get to family members, and/or depart a hazardous area. In addition to knowing all means of exit from a building, local street routes should also be known for the sake of community and regional evacuations emanating from weather related phenomenon like hurricanes, blizzards, and the like. This information is also helpful when dealing with issues stemming from disasters like explosions, train derailments, tanker leaks, plane crashes, or nuclear power plants.

As an example, some friends of mine were hunting in Argentina one year and they had a layover in Santiago, Chile. That night, February 27, 2010, as they lay in their beds fast asleep, an earthquake registering 8.8 on the Richter scale struck. The four-man hunting party, spread out on multiple floors of the hotel, awoke to their beds violently shaking, furniture toppling over, mirrors and artwork flying around the room. Each of these men had to navigate through the darkened and rapidly decaying building where they were now trapped. As they tried to exit via stairwells, they found the doors and doorjambs warped, twisted, and unable to be opened. Speaking only barely passable 'Spanglish,' each man was able to breach the wire-mesh inlaid security windows with the assistance of other hotel guests and a fire extinguisher. Once inside the stairwells, entire sections of stairs were missing. Quick thinking, communication, and teamwork allowed each man to marshal the other guests and traverse the stairwell until they were all able to evacuate the hotel.

Important Documents

In the event that there is a fire or flood, or some other calamity, befalling your home or apartment, it is important to have the originals of all your important documents stored in an easily accessible off-site location, preferably in a safe deposit box. Copies should be made for items like:

- Marriages License, Divorce Decree, Death Certificates
- Housing/Land Deeds, Vehicle Titles
- Mortgage/Rental Agreement Documents
- Social Security Cards, Birth Certificates, Passports
- Banking Account/Routing Numbers/Information
- Living Wills, Organ and Tissue Donation, DNR Statements
- Blood Types/Known Allergies
- Military Records (DD 214 and others)

When possible, certain documents can be scanned and miniaturized for placement in a purse or wallet. These are items like a marriage license and blood typing cards denoting each family member's blood type and any known allergies. The Social Security Card should already be credit card size. It also wouldn't be a bad idea to laminate the copies of all documents to protect these documents from harm. Some original documents may be laminated as well, but legally not all.

Family Emergency Planning

Questions six through nine all deal with emergency planning and discussion with your family.

Family Planning

Examples of a family emergency plan will require you to answer questions like:

- Does each family member know where to go in case there is a house fire?
- Is there a call tree in place if you have a larger, or extended, family?
- How are family members supposed to contact everyone if the cell towers are jammed?
- Do you have any specific instructions for your children or spouse that deviate from defined workplace, school, or community emergency plans?

Answer these questions and you will be ahead of about 90% of the population.

You don't need to be preparing for a massive financial collapse to have a conversation with your kids about safety and planning. For example, do you and your family have a plan in place if any of the following occur:

- House/apartment fire
- Flash flooding
- Tornado

I point to these three events because they can occur with little to no warning. If everyone knows what they are supposed to do, or where to go, panic is less likely to occur. As an example, my family and I have winnowed down our evacuation protocols to just two tasks – one task for each parent. My job is to get our daughters and dog out of the house while my wife is to grab the external hard drive from our computer. That's it. Everything else is insured, can be replaced, or is offsite.

Let's move on to certain style events that are outside of family and more in the natural disaster arena. Here's an example of natural disasters that, depending on where you are, could have easily moved you through the scale of minor, moderate, or major disruption:

During the planning of this book, the Gulf Coast and Southeastern United States were drilled repeatedly by hurricanes. I provide the following as examples of how quickly a known event, meaning an event you can see coming, can quickly transition all three of the disruption durations:

In 2016, Hurricane Matthew left over 2.5M households without power from Florida to North Carolina, destroyed the Caribbean, and killed 605 people. I called a few friends and family in the Carolinas to check on the situation during the height of the storm. Many said that there is, obviously, a lot of wind, rain, and flooding, but that there were also a high number of trees down. Twenty inches of rain in eight hours during the storm, coupled with eight to twelve inches of rain the previous week in central North Carolina, led to catastrophic devastation. The pine trees fared well due to their deep taproot, but the hardwoods dropped left and right. One family lost about three dozen hardwoods over their twenty acres. When I checked back in with them, they said they couldn't get out of their driveway for five days and power wasn't restored for twelve.

In 2017, over the span of forty-five days (late August through early October):

- Hurricane Harvey hit Texas/Louisiana (08/26/17 - 108 dead)
- Hurricane Irma hit Florida (09/10/17 - 146 dead)
- Hurricane Maria hit Puerto Rico (09/20/17 - 112 dead, revised to 2,975 on 08/28/18)
- Hurricane Nate hit Louisiana/Mississippi (10/08/17 - 45 dead)

Millions of families were without power, uprooted, and devastated. Their possessions were flooded, blown down, or washed away. Sadly, thousands of people, directly and indirectly, lost their lives to these storms. Now, most of these deaths were the result of failing to evacuate (where possible), shoddy building standards, poor planning, and even worse decision making (pre and post storm).

Reports say Puerto Rico didn't see the return of full power to the island for almost an entire year. An article titled *Puerto Rico: This is What Living in a 6 Month Blackout Looks Like* did a fairly decent job of detailing life on the island afterward. [Full URL: https://www.askaprepper.com/puerto-rico-this-is-what-living-in-a-6-month-blackout-looks-like].

I could provide additional articles about corruption and government malfeasance on that island, but I just want you to focus on living conditions and life after a major disruption. These weather-related issues are being called out because several of the hurricanes by-passed the minor disturbance level and went straight to the 'moderate' and 'major' disruption category. Knowing what they experienced, it begs some of the following questions.

> Do you have enough of the following to last _**at least**_ two solid weeks for everyone living in your home, pets included?

- Consumable Supplies
- Food and Water
- Fuel
  - For a vehicle to go 50-100 miles (one-way, double for round-trip) to get supplies
  - For the portable generator (assuming you have one)
  - For the house generator (e.g. Generac, assuming you have one that is not on a city feed – long term issue)
  - For cooking meals and boiling water (propane, white, wood, or charcoal - assuming you don't have a natural gas burning stove/hot water heater)
  - For the space heater (typically kerosene)
  - For the fireplace, wood burning stove, wood burning furnace (i.e. firewood)
- Medications

Depending on your needs, if you flesh out the Consumable Supplies, you might add:

- Batteries (varying sizes)
- Candles (long burning), matches, lighters
- Dishwashing soap/scrubber
- Feminine supplies
- Laundry detergent
- Paper plates, cups, plastic cutlery
- Pots/pans
- Soap, shampoo, deodorant
- Toilet Paper
- Toothbrushes, toothpaste, floss
- Tub/clothesline (for washing/drying clothes)

Granted, food and water are consumable products too, but I've made those separate line item categories for the simple fact that you need those two items to live and survive. These other items are just for comfort.

When it comes to a whole house generator (ex. Generac), I'd like to have you consider two things:

1. If the city is without power and your whole house generator is hooked into a city fed gas line, there is the possibility that you lose your gas feed due to a lack of power to the pressurization pumps at the pumping station.
2. A week is just about enough time for people to start panicking and doing questionable things… things they never would have thought themselves capable of doing prior to the event. Two weeks without reliable food, water, and electricity and you're bound to have a run in or two with someone more desperate than you.

I'm drawing your attention to these typically un-thought of details because, for as long as the natural gas (or propane, or diesel) can power the generator, a home lit up like Christmas against a backdrop of sheer darkness is a tempting target. We'll get to the concept of discretion and security a little later.

For me, the preliminary questions and various scenarios present in this section are enough of a reason to begin seriously thinking about preparing to prepare.

What do you think?

Vehicle Planning

When it comes to travel, every car should have a basic emergency breakdown bag/tote, complete with first aid kit. For example, each car should have the following at all times:

- Dried Kindling (wood/moss/lint)/Fire Starter Cubes
- First Aid Kit (robust)
- Fix-a-Flat Tire Sealant
- Flashlight/Lantern
- Functioning Spare Tire
- Fuses
- Jumper Cables
- Matches/Lighter
- Motor Oil
- Paracord (100-200 feet)
- Portable Air Pump
- Putty Strips (high temp for gas tank/radiator leaks)
- Radiator Fluid
- Rain Suit
- Reflective Hazard Triangle
- Reflective Vest
- Roadside Flares
- Solar Blanket
- Tarp
- Tow Straps
- Water
- Windshield Washer Fluid

All of the items noted (except for the spare tire, obviously) should fit snugly in a medium sized tote. In addition, if all items *are* in a tote, it will help prevent spillage and leakage.

If you or any member of your family drives long stretches in remote areas, you might also want to consider some elements of a 'get home' bag/kit. In additional to the breakdown bin, these contents might consist of:

- One Man Tent
- -20 degree Sleeping Bag
- Food (3-days to 1-week)
- Single Burner Stove (propane/butane with tank)

After that, you need to think seasonally. Meaning, as fall approaches, grab a bag of kitty litter or sand and the bag with the tire chains (if applicable to your location or route) and put them in the trunk as winter approaches. The extra weight will also aid you in traction.

Your circumstance may necessitate that the bag is more robust because you travel greater distances on a daily basis. Alternatively, perhaps, you are never more than ten-miles from home at any given point during the course of the day. If that is the case, and your route is urban, then perhaps you could go with an even smaller bag.

What I've just described is, for better or worse, a vehicle repair bag (tote) which addresses the potential for being stranded in a remote area. Technically, you could call it a 'Get Home Bag.' Pack whatever you like in there (or follow the list provided), but the idea behind this is that it contains whatever you might need, by season, to safely get you home *in your vehicle*. Now, if you are on foot, for whatever reason, a 'Get Home Bag' has a completely different connotation. This will be discussed later.

Home Maintenance

A factor that cannot be overlooked when it comes to pre-disruption planning is keeping up with the maintenance on your home. This is as straight forward of a topic as it comes.

Assuming you've been in your home, or at least that region, for some time, you have a general idea as to when you need to be on the lookout for any weather-related calamity.

For example, if you're anywhere near tornado alley, you should know that peak tornado season runs from late spring to mid-summer. If you're anywhere near the Atlantic or Gulf coasts, you should know that hurricane season runs June 1 through November 30 each year and that it generally peaks in late August through September.

Therefore, if you are near one of these places that experiences extreme weather at specific times of the year, you can have things prepared and at the ready. Meaning, if you are in or near tornado alley, make sure your storm cellar is accessible at all times. The doors to the cellar should open, close, and lock easily for quick ingress and egress. The defined space is stocked and replenished as needed and appropriate with the necessary items required to endure the time spent in the cellar. Because tornadoes can't really be planned for giving their spontaneous nature, you need to have everything already in place in the cellar.

The same is true for those near the coasts.

Because hurricanes can be prepared for days in advance, those potentially affected by hurricanes should have the plywood already measured and cut to board up windows and doors. They should also have a healthy supply of empty sandbags, batteries, fuel, water, and food at the ready. You do not want to be part of the unprepared locusts that are going to strip all supplies from the area at the last minute.

Now, beyond preparing for calamities that have a defined season, you should keep a constant vigil for things that need to be addressed on the home itself for routine day-to-day living.

I'd highly recommend enlisting any energy provider's program for a 'home energy audit.' In most cases, the bigger energy providers have a program whereby they'll send a representative to your home with fans, thermal imagers, and assorted temporary plastic and evaluate your homes overall energy efficiency.

During the energy audit, they'll determine:

- An overall efficiency rating for you homes ability to keep and retain heat, air-conditioning
- Any insufficient insulation locations in walls and attics
- Any draft locations where you're losing heat or A/C
- Any doors and windows that are warped or not functioning properly

Once you know where the issues lie (doors, windows, insulation, or any combination thereof), you can address each over time as your budget allows, but don't dawdle. The longer it takes the more money you're bleeding.

Additionally, after every major storm and/or twice a year, at a minimum, you should inspect your home for the following and address any deficiencies as needed when encountered:

- Crumbling mortar in joints (especially the chimney stack)
- Air gaps where bugs or critters can enter foundations, windows, doors, attics, and under decks
- Loose or missing siding
- Loose or missing gutters, down spouts, and drain tile connections
- Loose or missing roofing material
- Proper venting from bathrooms, laundry, and kitchen fans
- Cracked, broken, or missing glass
- Snake drain tiles and sanitary piping
- Snake slow drains from tubs, showers, sinks (as needed)

By tackling any issues before hand, you'll have that much more peace of mind and the time spent without electricity due to a disruption is that much easier to bear. Additionally, to make yourself comfortable when you have electricity, you should have your mechanicals (furnace, A/C, hot water heater, chimney, etc.) inspected every year by qualified professionals. My suggestion for these inspections would be to have them inspected out of season to maximize cost savings. Additionally, the chimney isn't necessarily a mechanical but needs to be cleaned based on use if you're burning wood regularly. The same is true for any wood burning stove piping.

Blood Type

The last item in the 'Everyday Needs' list dealt with blood type. If, in the unfortunate event that someone sustains an injury, knowing your family members' blood types can speed up triage and care if they are transported to a hospital. This knowledge can literally save someone's life. This information is doubly important if you are in a secluded location and medical attention is hours away or on the off-chance society has collapsed.

Medical Blood-Type Transfusion Xref:

Blood Type	Receive From	Donate To
O+	O+, O-	O+, A+, B+, AB+
O-	O-	Universal Donor
A+	A+, A-, O+, O-	A+, AB+
A-	A-, O-	A+, A-, AB+, AB-
B+	B+, B-, O+, O-	B+, AB+
B-	B-, O-	B+, B-, AB+, AB-
AB+	Universal Recipient	AB+
AB-	AB-, A-, B-, O-	AB+, AB-

Now that we've taken a deep dive into these questions, hopefully, you are able to plan more effectively for potential issues dealing with work, school, and your community.

Chapter 3 - Minor Disruptions

As was previously stated, a minor disruption is an event that lasts from one day to one week. The bulk of these disruptions are generally going to be weather related but it could also be a fluke like some construction crew could dig through an underground line too.

The rule of three states that, a human can go:

- Three minutes without oxygen
- Three days without water, and
- Three weeks without food.

Now, when it comes to basic needs, per the rule of three's, food and water are necessary. Beyond that, the next priority for most of us is to either get warm or cool off. That's where fire and shelter enter the discussion. Therefore, I have grouped these four items together (water, food, fire, shelter) under the heading, *The Basics*. In this Chapter, we will discuss, and I will list out, what the 'basics' might entail for a minor disruption.

As a primer to a discussion on the basics, I should at least mention the Federal Emergency Management Agency, or FEMA.

Until recently, FEMA stated that every family should have at least three days' worth of food and water on hand, at all times, in the event of an emergency. Now, FEMA says it's broke (financially) and everyone is, more or less, on their own. The issues surrounding FEMA's demise are outlined in this December 19, 2017 CNN article titled: *Hellish Summer of Hurricanes Smashes FEMA* [Full URL: http://www.cnn.com/2017/12/19/politics/summer-of-hurricanes-broke-fema-weir/index.html].

The first question regarding FEMA's recommendation for three days of food and water would be, why. Why only three days? Well, this was most likely due to, or based in part on, some bean counter's estimates. When the Agency was created in 1978-1979, the federal government figured that, no matter how bad the tragedy, given the resources of the United States, aid could be brought in by air, sea, or land in three days or less.

Good theory... didn't work on the Gulf Coast after Hurricane Katrina (2005) or Puerto Rico (2017). Now, nearly two decades since Katrina, the global supply chain is even more entrenched in our modern societies. As a result, global pandemic disruptions like

COViD-19 (2020) are creating food and supply shortages and the inevitable price gouging that comes along with it.

My personal position is that every household should, at a minimum, have at least a two-week supply of food and water for each family member, pets included, on hand at all times. A two-week supply will get you through a 'minor disruption' with a week to spare and about half of the maximum time allotted for a 'moderate disruption.' Two-weeks of water, food, fuel, supplies, etc. is easy to store, doesn't take up much room, and provides a fair amount of peace of mind. This is the best place to start in my opinion.

As a child growing up in northern Virginia, we were subject to blizzards, hurricanes, and ice storms. As a teenager living in southern North Carolina, we removed blizzards from the mix and added dangerous and oppressive heat waves to the hurricanes and ice storms. Good times. Now, as an adult with a family of my own in the Midwest, the heat waves are dialed back a bit and the occasional hurricane remnant appears more as a 'derecho' wind storm with little rain to speak of. However, now I get to add the blizzards back into the mix AND add the fun of being at the northeastern end of tornado alley.

If you just look at the weather that can potentially affect you, why wouldn't you consider being prepared?

Pre-Disruption Planning – Minor

If you, like most people, feel that a minor disruption is all you need to plan for, then consider using the preliminary list of items below as a starting point for the things to consider having on-hand. Please bear in mind; this is not an exhaustive list. Your location, situation, dietary restrictions, medical conditions, etc. may dictate a more specific list and deviate from the noted items.

As was mentioned in the previous chapter, the list went something like this, but with some notable additions broken out to provide more detail:

- The Basics (food, water, fire, shelter)
  - See *The Basics* section
- Batteries
  - Various sizes
  - Rechargeable
- Cooking
  - Dishwashing soap/scrubber
  - Grill (propane/charcoal/firewood)
  - Paper plates, plastic cups and cutlery
  - Pots/pans
  - Stove (single/double burner with fuel)
  - Tubs for washing dishes
- Electricity (generation)
  - Extension cords (to power refrigerators, freezers, pumps)
  - Gas generator
  - Mini solar (recharge phones/batteries)
- First Aid Kid (robust)
- Fuel
  - Butane
  - Charcoal
  - Diesel
  - Firewood
  - Kerosene
  - Mixed fuel (for chainsaws)
  - Propane
  - Unleaded
  - White
- Hygiene
  - Deodorant

- o   Hand Sanitizer
- o   Pads/tampons/Diva Cup
- o   Shampoo
- o   Soap
- o   Toothbrush/toothpaste
- o   Toilet paper
- Laundry
  - o   Clothesline and pins
  - o   Detergent/soap
  - o   Hanging rack
  - o   Spin dryer/laundry wringer
  - o   Washboard with tub
- Lighting
  - o   Candles (long burning)
  - o   Coleman lanterns (with spare mantles)
  - o   Flashlights
  - o   Lighters/matches
- Medications
  - o   Over the counter pain, burn, anti-itch, antibiotic cream
  - o   Prescription (to include birth control pills and condoms)
  - o   Supplements
  - o   Vitamins
- Sleeping bags (-20 degree)
- Weather radio

As we progress into the 'Moderate' and 'Major' disruption durations, you will notice that the list of concepts, and skillsets, will grow as will the quantities for the previously listed. However, for a 'Minor' disruption, the previous list should get you started. Adjust your list to your needs. It should be noted that, regardless of the season that the event (disruption) occurred, the list provided assumes you are still in your home.

The Basics

As we discuss 'The Basics,' it is important to keep in mind that these are suggestions based on experiences I've personally encountered or situations that were described to me by others that lived through the disruption. I have purposefully limited this discussion to the four key fundamentals comprising this topic: water, food, fire, and shelter.

Your location and personal situation will determine the list of potential disruptions, its duration, and the method to which you address the issues. Therefore, take what I have written, use it as a starting point, and customize it to your needs. There are no absolutes when it comes to planning for a disruption of any duration. In addition, I've decided to start with water because, if we utilize the rule of three's, water ranks higher on the needs list than food.

Let's dig into the basics of water, food, fire, and shelter.

Water

Water is an essential part to any preparedness planning. Your body needs it to maintain a great number of functions, your family needs it to clean dishes and clothes, it's required in meal prep/clean-up, and your plants (garden) absolutely have to have it.

According to the Mayo Clinic, on average, an adult living in a temperate environment needs about half a gallon of water a day, or eight 8-ounce glasses (64 ounces). Over the course of a day, an adult will ingest about one gallon of water via food and drink. Please note that your activity level, environment, and/or location within that environment, may require you to have more water in a day. If we just focus on drinking water, and we use the typical nuclear family of four as an example, the math looks like this:

- Adults
  - 0.5 gal per day x 7 days = 3.5 gal x 2 adults = 7 gal per week
- Children (13+)
  - 0.5 gal per day x 7 days = 3.5 gal x 2 children = 7 gal per week
- Children (12-)
  - 0.25 gal per day x 7 days = 1.75 gal x 2 children = 3.5 gal per week

Most, not all, families tend to have their children close in age. If this is the case for you, and the children are teenagers (13 and over), then you have the following totals:

- 7 gal for 2 adults + 7 gal for 2 children = 14 gal per week per family of four

If the children are not teenagers (12 and under), then you get:

- 7 gal for 2 adults + 3.5 gal for 2 children = 10.5 gal per week per family of four

If the last child was of the, 'hey, how did that happen' variety, then your math is as follows:

7 gal for 2 adults + 3.5 gal for 1 child (13+) + 1.75 for 1 child (12-) = 12.25 gal per week per family of four

If you have pets, you need to account for their needs as well. Cats are easy. They only require about a cup of water a day. Assuming you have two cats, the math looks like this:

- 1 C per day x 7 days = ~ 0.5 gal x 2 cats = ~ 1 gal per week

A dog on the other hand, generally requires 0.5 to 1-ounce of water per pound. Therefore, if you have a healthy sixty-five-pound lab, you will need the following:

- 0.5 gal (64 oz.) per day x 7 days = 3.5 gal per week

You *must* account for the needs of your pets for any disruption duration. Therefore, in addition to the 10.5-14 gallons the family needs for the minor disruption, you'll also need to add an extra 1-gallon for the cats and/or an extra 3.5-gallons of water for the dog.

So how do you solve this problem?

The simplest and easiest method would be to store cases of water. Sam's Club, as an example, offers a 40-pack case of water for $2.98. Each bottle contains 16.9 ounces of water. This means that the average adult/teenager will need to drink just under four bottles of water a day to stay hydrated. Unfortunately, they've recently started disclosing that one of their added ingredients is sodium. In order to find a bottler that doesn't add sodium, you might need to spend more. Regardless, here's the water bottle math for the case lot coming from Sam's Club:

1/2 gal = 64 oz / 16.9 oz = 3.78 bottles of water

For convenience, if we round up and say that the adult/teenager drank 4 bottles a day, the 40-pack of water will last 10 days. This clears the 7-day max duration for a minor disturbance. As a result, for $15.00 + tax (5 cases) you will have provided enough water for your nuclear family and its pets to endure a minor disturbance… but now you have cases of water you need to store somewhere. You also have to remember to drink, replenish, and rotate the cases as water does eventually turn.

Isn't there an easier way?

Well, yes and no. When it comes to water, you really have three potential options. The first two options are viable for those on a city water feed and/or on well water. If you have well water though, the third option needs to be studied, researched, and resolved before the disruption.

1. Store water pre-bottled in various sized containers and take on the task of maintaining a constant stockpile of five cases (see previously mathematical example), or
2. Maintain a higher degree of vigilance for your surroundings and capture the water when needed.

Did you know that an average bathtub will hold approximately 35-50 gallons of water? Larger tubs, like soaking tubs and freestanding tubs, hold almost double that at 60-80 gallons. Jacuzzi tubs go to about 100-120 gallons.

Knowing this, you could purchase a Water Bob for the same cost as the cases of water. The Water Bob system is a giant reusable food grade plastic bladder capable of holding up to 100 gallons of water from the spigot in your bathtub. In an emergency, simply place it in the tub and fill it up. [Full URL: https://www.waterbob.com].

What else can I do?

Well, there are water filtration systems called:

- Big Berkey [Full URL: https://www.berkeywater.com/big-berkey-system-2-25-gal/]
- Alexapure [Full URL: https://www.mypatriotsupply.com/water_filtration_s/181.htm]

These filtration systems have high startup costs in my opinion, $265 for the Berkey and $250 for the Alexapure. Both systems also require filter replacement ($50-$100 per filter) after a specified number of gallons (~ 5,000 gallons) have been purified. Lastly, both systems require that you provide the water to be filtered.

Another stored water option might be to have a bottled water delivery service like many offices that provides multiple 5-gallon containers to sit in a dispenser (water cooler). This, obviously, is not the most cost effective method as each 5-gallon container (640 oz) delivered is about $6-$8 and requires the rental of the water cooler stand. To purchase the stand is around $75-$100. A battery operated pump that fits over the 5-gallon water bottle neck is a viable solution as well and is about $15.

Some newer homes, and older retrofitted homes, now have tank less water heaters. Most of these are 110V and can be plugged into an extension cord. This could be a real lifesaver if you still have your city water feed and a generator. However, this isn't a cheap option.

Water harvesting from roof structures and underground cistern storage are also a viable sources for water and can be utilized pre-disruption. These topics are discussed at length in Chapter 4.

The third option is for those that are on well water. If you are on a well and don't have power during a minor disturbance, this poses a serious problem.

3. Well users need to address this shortcoming by installing or using one of the following options (video and/or article links provided):
   - Gas generator (to power the pump)
     - https://www.youtube.com/watch?v=tLNZMY16044
   - Battery backup (to power the pump)
     - (Part 1)
       https://www.youtube.com/watch?v=J1rrgxM9Nn8
     - (Part 2)
       https://www.youtube.com/watch?v=7nsMR9TmUXY
   - Solar Pump Kit
     - https://www.rpssolarpumps.com/
   - Hand pump (well head without a motor)
     - https://www.youtube.com/watch?v=It3CvoRxmmE
   - Hand pump (well head with a motor)
     - https://www.youtube.com/watch?v=GIRAm5gaUhg
     - https://www.motherearthnews.com/diy/hand-pump-electric-well-zmaz84zloeck

There are many possible solutions to your water issues. Do your research and go with one or two based on your needs and your budget. That being said, we will discuss more advanced electrical and water concepts in the Moderate and Major disruption chapters.

Lastly, in addition to the two water filtration systems I noted previously, you also need to be mindful of other means for water purification. Depending on your situation, you might want to keep a healthy stock of the following options:

- Bleach
- Old towels/t-shirts
- Purification tablets/iodine
- Britta/Pur (pitchers/water bottles and several spare filters for each)

Food

When people ask me for advice regarding their desire to begin preparing to prepare, I generally provide the following response:

1. Answer the 'What are you preparing for?' question, and;
2. Regardless of that answer, start small.

Starting small is sound advice because your intention may very well be to prepare for the absolute worst, a 'major disruption.' Your finances however, will probably dictate otherwise. The good news is that when it comes to food, as it pertains to a minor disruption, you have a wide variety of options. For example, you could buy:

- Extras of family favorites and then set those aside
- An assortment of freeze dried vacuum sealed packages
- Large #10 cans containing a variety of options
- Canning supplies and can your own food
- Dehydrator
- Vacuum sealer
- Food grade barrels and package your own food

The list could go on and on, but you get the point. My recommendation is to literally start at the top of the list and work your way down as your skills progress or your preparedness desires change.

Now, for a minor disruption, the amount of physical labor associated with the recovery effort *should* be relatively minor. You'll probably be doing to some debris clean-up for a day or so, maybe work a chainsaw for a couple of hours, or perhaps you'll have to remove plywood from windows and doors, maybe even lend a hand to a neighbor. This is very different from a 'major disruption' where you are literally laboring to survive.

I am mentioning physical labor under the heading of 'Food' because you need to understand that with labor comes caloric burn. This is important because the more physically demanding the labor, the more calories your body is going to need to replenish itself and recover.

So, where do you start?

Let's start with what you know, and where... your grocery store. This is a good place to start because you already shop there. In addition, there is the added benefit of cost reduction via coupons, rewards programs, and the added potential benefit for fuel cost savings.

Before we get to that though, I do need to mention something that is very important when it comes to planning for minor to major disruptions as it pertains to food, and that is shelf life.

If we are working on the premise that you are preparing for an emergency, then we have to accept the premise that, generally speaking, emergencies are rare. If emergencies weren't rare, then that would just be life. Now, because we are looking for 'ease of use,' let's discuss food items that can be stored short-term.

Short-Term Storage Foods

The following items are ideal for short-term emergencies and carry a 2 to 5-year shelf life:

- Canned Meats
- Canned Tuna
- Canned Vegetables & Fruits
- Coffee
- Dried herbs and spices
- Freeze dried meals
- Freeze dried snacks
- Hard Candy
- Meal Replacement Bars
- Peanut Butter
- Powdered milk
- Ramen Noodles
- Tea

The items noted have a decent shelf life so they will stay fresh for a fair amount of time. The key to short-term food for an emergency is to have food on hand that requires very little cooking, can be eaten without any, or very little, preparation at all, and are inexpensive to replace as you use and replenish your stock (stock rotation).

Don't overdo it with Ramen though. There is a lot of sodium in those flavor packets. Consider only using half or a quarter of the seasoning packet for the noodles and saving the un-used portion to flavor something else later. Also, a new study was just released that states Ramen is a contributor to memory and Alzheimer's related issues. This relationship is not fully proven, but here's a URL for you to review: http://healthycures.org/noodles-cause-chronic-inflammation-weight-gain-alzheimers-parkinsons-disease

Additional Items

Some additional food related items that can be comforting, have multiple uses, and could prove beneficial regardless of duration are:

- Apple Cider Vinegar
  - Cleaning
  - Cooking
  - Medical – contains antibiotic properties
- Baking Soda
  - Cleaning
  - Odor absorption
  - Toothpaste
- Raw Honey
  - Natural sweetener
  - Antibiotic properties
  - Helpful with slow healing wounds

In summary, start small with a few cans or bags of whatever you like from the grocery store. Use these pre-disruption moments to teach yourself new skills and methods for cooking and storing.

Here are some suggestions for you to try:

- Cook a meal starting with a bag of dry beans (hint: soak them in water overnight first)
- Cook multiple types of rice and see which variety appeals more (I like to add raisins to wild long grain rice)
- Cook the beans/rice in a variety of ways with and without electricity to see which one is the most practical for minor and moderate disturbances

Long-term food storage will be discussed later on and can possibly be used during a short-term emergency. However, the converse isn't always true.

The last thing I'd like to note when it comes to food is electricity. If you have a lot of food that is refrigerated (some medications require refrigeration as well) or frozen, you **_need_** to have a plan to keep these devices running. For this reason, you need to seriously consider a gas generator that has multiple outlets if a whole house generator is not an viable financial option right away. At a minimum, you need to know that you can at least load up all of the food in coolers and take everything, possibly the freezers as well, somewhere that has electricity available.

Fire

Basic preparedness dictates that you should have some means of making a fire handy at all times.

But what does that mean?

Well, aside from primitive skills like using a bow drill, I'd recommend the following materials be on hand at all times regardless of the disruption duration:

- Bic Lighters
- Strike Anywhere Matches
- Zippo Lighter

You can get a 3-pack of strike anywhere matches with 300 matches per box on Amazon for about $12.50. The Bic lighters can be small pocket size or long stick lighters. Sticking with Amazon, you can get 12 pocket size lighters or 4 stick lighters for about $14.00. Eventually though, the Bic lighters will run out of fuel and they aren't easily refilled which is why I also added the Zippo lighter. The Zippo lighter is refillable but requires a flint. Amazon lists an all-in-one starter kit, which contains the lighter, 4 oz. bottle of fuel, and 6 extra flint for $17.00.

You can purchase additional wick material (5-pack for $7), fuel (4 oz 2-pack for $9), and flint (6-pack w/ 6-flint each for $7) individually to have spares or for barter as well. Combination packages of wick and flint, or wick and fuel, or wick, fuel, and flint are available as well.

Now that you have the ability to create fire, what are you going to light?

For a minor disruption, this is most likely going to be a lantern, camping stove (one or two-burner), a gas grill (assuming it doesn't have a built in ignitor), charcoal grill, or a wood burning fire pit.

As an example, in 2007, the remnants of a hurricane blew through the Midwest dropping very little rain but packing 60-70 mph winds. It knocked out our power for a week. I learned a lot about fire during that week.

Don't make the same mistakes I did before I started seriously getting prepared. If you don't have the ability to make fire, chances are incredibly high that many other people don't either. They *will* beat you to any store that is open like a horde of locusts.

In fact, I learned several lessons that week, and to be honest, not all of them were good.

- Lesson #1: Always, always, always have a spare 25# propane cylinder (LP tank) extra that is full and ready for use (2 spare tanks would be better).
- Lesson #2: Have 2-3 bags of charcoal on hand, if there is an issue with any gas grills or camping stoves.
- Lesson #3: Kindling in any form is better than no kindling.

The second and third lessons prove out a time-honored tradition when it comes to preparedness, which is to have a back up to your back up.

Things went so horribly wrong for me that week that it literally jump-started my preparedness journey. During that week, I was forced to light a fire in my wood burning fire pit and break out my Coleman tripod grill and lantern hanger (Amazon $25.00) just to boil water and prepare meals. Ever since that week, I have always maintained the following fire related items:

- 6 bags of charcoal
- 6 25# propane tanks*
  - 1 tank each for grill, gas fire pit, patio heater
  - 1 spare tank for each
- 3 1-gal bags of dryer lint
- 12 16 oz. Propane Fuel Cylinders
- Bic Lighters (pocket and stick)
- Camp fire grate
- Cord of firewood (8'x4'x4')**
- Galvanized tub of fallen sticks and twigs
- Weber Fire Starting Cubes
- 4 gallons of white fuel (2-burner stove, lantern)
- Zippo lighter (with extra fuel, flint, and wick)

* You can procure used 25# propane tanks ($10-$25) on many apps and websites like Craig's List, Offer Up (formerly LetGo), Mercari, eBay, and Facebook Marketplace (to name a few). My wife is a member of several community-based Buy/Sell/Trade sites as well. Additionally, propane tanks are stamped with a manufacturing date and are good for refilling for up to 15 years. Be sure to look for this date on the collar of the cylinder before buying as they may have already expired.

Taking the tanks to a refilling station (mine is at a U-Haul rental facility) costs about half as much ($12-$15) as opposed to exchanging the tanks at your local gas station (~ $25). You *will* have to exchange any expired tanks so check that manufacturing date, as propane refillers will not fill an expired tank. Call around ahead of time because, just like gas for your car, propane refilling is charged on a per gallon basis. Currently, the best price I've found within 10-miles of me is $3.00 per gallon.

** Full, 1/2, and 1/4 cords of firewood ($50-$150) can also be found of the websites previously noted. Most firewood sellers will deliver a 1/2 and full cord of firewood for a modest fee (sometimes free), but you'll likely have to pick up the 1/4 cord. This, of course, assumes that you don't have the means to cut and split your own firewood. Additionally, do occasional online searches in those sites for the term 'free firewood.' I've filled an 8x4 rack for free several times this way, you just have to be willing to go get it.

Shelter

When it comes to shelter, for our purposes throughout the *Minor Disruption* chapter, I have assumed that you are still residing in your house, apartment, or condominium. This is referred to as sheltering in place.

However, what if you weren't or couldn't remain in your home? What if friends or family didn't have the space or inclination to take in short-term boarders (because that's what you are at this point)? What if there weren't any hotel or motel rooms available?

Now what?

Well, now, you're effectively camping, or in a government shelter.

There are other options before you pitch a tent or accept government assistance though. For example, I've had friends and neighbors get their motor home, fifth wheel, and/or pop-up camper out of storage to use in this situation. Unfortunately, due to the distance between us, I couldn't offer assistance to others so they had to break out their tents. Those that didn't even have tents went to designated emergency shelters. I can say that those that have accepted government assistance and/or used shelters never did so again. Once they were back on their feet, they did everything they could to be better prepared.

If you're in the camping category, and depending on the season and your situation, you'll want to have some options. The first thing you're going to want to do is salvage as much of your prepared supplies from your damaged home, if possible. At a minimum, you'll want to have:

- 1 or 2-burner camping stove with fuel
- 500' Paracord/rope
- Folding chairs
- Folding tables
- Freeze dried food
- Hammock(s)
- Pop-up canopy (10x10 or 12x12)
- Sleeping bag for each person (rated to -20 degrees)
- Stakes
- Tent(s) (4-season preferred in 1-man, 2-man, or family size)
- Tarps (various sizes)
- Sleeping pads (foam or inflatable)
- Water

The last thing I'd like to mention regarding shelter is electricity as it pertains to sump and well pumps.

If your home is uninhabitable, then perhaps this isn't a major concern in that moment. However, for arguments sake, say you are still in your home but you've lost power for the full one-week duration described as a minor disruption. If your home has a sump pump, you will need to figure out a way to keep the pump(s) powered. This is more of a concern if the reason for the power outage was associated with rain and/or flooding in your area. If you don't, you'll be adding a rather unenviable task to your list of things to do when the power returns. This thought process could also be applied to your well pump if you use well water. Access to clean drinking water is the highest priority regardless of duration.

Your first option for the sump pump is to have a battery backup installed. The bigger the better. The biggest ones are rated to handle up to 40-50 hours without electricity if running modestly. Unfortunately, if it's running constantly, it will only last about 16 hours. The only option after that is a gas powered generator and an extension cord to power the pumps. Unfortunately, this is likely your only option for a well pump. This potential solution assumes that an extension cord will work for a well pump. Gaining access to drinking water in an emergency is the highest priority and an issue you will need to solve.

I wouldn't recommend relying exclusively on a solar backup in this instance. While it is a solid back-up, the weather may hamper its effectiveness or may have damaged the system. Most sump pumps are rated at 1/2 horsepower. Well pumps, on the other hand, are rated based on a combination of the well depth and the designed/desired gallons per minute (gpm). Any solar solution will need to be rated to handle the pump's defined electrical load. Please review the *Electricity* section in Chapter 4 for more information on generators, fuel needs, and solar options.

* * *

Additional topics that you'll want to address and/or consider (E.g. electricity, fuel, laundry, long-term food storage, bartering) in a minor disturbance can be found in *Chapter 4* and *Chapter 5*. While some of the noted examples can be useful in a minor disturbance, I've tried to keep like information together for placement in the most appropriate duration level chapter.

Chapter 4 - Moderate Disruptions

By my own definition, a moderate disruption could be any event that lasts from a week to a month. A disruption of this length will require a greater degree of diligence to overcome. It will be tempting to look at this duration (4-weeks max) and say, 'I'll just quadruple what I plan on doing for a minor disruption (one week).' Or, for those of you heeding my advice to have at least a two-week stash to say, 'I'll just double that.'

Unfortunately, it's not as easy as that. Cost is usually a major hurdle to overcome for this 'just double it' or 'quadruple it' approach. Then, after that, space becomes a concern as well. Additionally, now that we are looking at spending nearly a month without basic services, you need to start seriously considering, or re-considering, your current location and security.

Pre-Disruption Planning – Moderate

Planning for a moderate disruption requires more, well, planning. This is because the duration could conceivably last an entire month. As was noted in the *Chapter 2 – Pre-Disruption Planning* and in the *Pre-Disruption Planning – Minor* section of Chapter 3, I recommended a whole host of items from documents to vehicle preparedness and basic non-food supplies. For the sake of brevity, I won't repeat them here.

However, in *Chapter 4 – Moderate Disruptions*, I will expand on a few of the items I listed in the previous chapters, namely electricity and fuel. Chapter 4 also will build on the concept of The Basics that we've previously discussed and start a discussion around gardens, tools, and security.

So, let's dig in and start upping our game on the Basics.

Water

As we discussed in *The Basics* section of Chapter 3, water is the most needed, and valuable, asset. When the duration is more than a few days (minor disruption), everything about water comes into play. That means your ability to locate, capture, and store water reserves as well as the ability to filter and purify water.

I hope that you have at least some of your water needs stored already either through bottled water or a Water Bob. Assuming that you do, you can supplement your water needs several ways.

Water Harvesting

Harvesting rainwater is a concept I've adhered to for many years. To get started, I managed to find a used rain barrel on Craig's List for $75.00 and then attached it to my downspout. The decorative ones that are designed to look like a barrel can cost anywhere from $100.00 - $200.00 new. Regular food grade barrels without any decorative features to make them look like an actual barrel cost less, usually around $75.00. Once you've procured the barrel(s), you'll need a gutter-connecting kit (diverter) as well as an overflow pipe. These are available at home improvement stores and online for cheap ($15.00-$25.00).

For our uses, I use my rain barrels for the gardens exclusively. In a minor or moderate disruption however, where water is the most valuable commodity, I would be able to utilize some of these stored gallons for anything I desired. The caveat is that if any of the water is being used for food prep or drinking water, the water needs to be boiled first.

I'll say that again, any water that has been collected from a roof (asphalt shingle, metal, tin, etc.) <u>must be boiled</u> before use in food prep or as drinking water!

Rain barrels come in all shapes, sizes, and colors. Most are 50-55 gallons and are made out of food grade plastic. As I noted earlier, if you don't care if they look like an actual barrel, then you can realize some definite cost savings. If money wasn't a hurdle, I'd prefer the slimmer design of the Rainwater H2OG [Full URL: http://www.rainwaterhog.com/], but they are about $370.00 per 50-gallon container.

Here's a tip when it comes to utilizing rain barrels. The higher you can get them off the ground the better. Gravity is what is going to create the pressure needed for watering. For this reason, consider stacking the barrels in a DIY rack of some kind. There are plenty of images, designs, and plans to view online.

Once I got the hang of the rain barrel concept, and understood that gravity makes everything work better, I was able to add additional barrels to the system. This was accomplished easily by simply attaching one barrel to another via PVC piping. There are barrel connect kits available as well for $10.00-$20.00.

Now, before you go crazy and start cutting your downspouts and installing diverters, you need to know how much rainwater you can collect. Here's the math:

- Catchment Area x Rainfall Depth x 0.623 Conversion Fraction = Harvested Water (gallons)

Take my house for example. I have three rooflines to account for. They are marked on the following image as "OP," "1s FR/FRG," and "2s FR/B" respectively. You can find similar information and diagrams for your home on your county auditor website. The abbreviations stand for Open Porch (OP), 1 Story Frame (1s FR/FRG), and 2 Story Frame (2s FR/B).

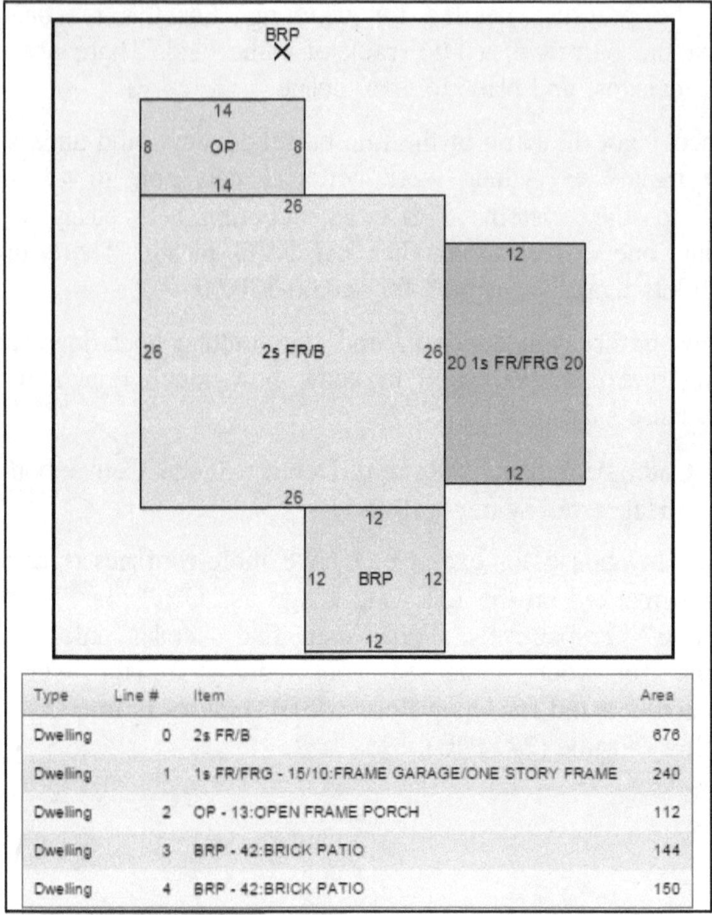

Type	Line #	Item	Area
Dwelling	0	2s FR/B	676
Dwelling	1	1s FR/FRG - 15/10:FRAME GARAGE/ONE STORY FRAME	240
Dwelling	2	OP - 13:OPEN FRAME PORCH	112
Dwelling	3	BRP - 42:BRICK PATIO	144
Dwelling	4	BRP - 42:BRICK PATIO	150

Based on the dimensions, my catchment area is as follows (and it's in the table beneath the image):

- OP = 112 sq ft

- 1s FR/FRG = 240 sq ft

- 2s FR/B = 676 sq ft

This gives me a catchment area of 1,028 sq. feet (112 + 240 + 676 = 1,028).

However, this isn't entirely true because my roof is angled. This math would only work if my roof were flat. Additionally, the measurements noted in the auditor website image are for the foundation of the home. My home, and yours, likely has angled roofs and overhangs. If I'm exacting, my main roof is a 28' wide square, not 26'. The ridge is 12' above the lowest point (gutter) and bisects the 28' measurement horizontally.

Knowing that an angled roof is two right angle triangles back to back, and because we know the length (28 / 2 = 14) and the height (12') of each triangle, all we need to do is use this mathematic formula ($a^2 + b^2 = c^2$) to find the hypotenuse (the angle which is where the shingles are):

$$14^2 \ (L) + 12^2 \ (H) = c^2 \ \rightarrow \ 196 + 144 = 340 \ \rightarrow \ \sqrt{340} = 18.44$$

Now that I know the hypotenuse (18.44') and the length (28'), the math gets easy.

28' (L) x 18.44' (hypotenuse) = 516.32 sq. ft. per each side of the roof → the math for the entire roof (both sides) would be 516.32 x 2 = 1,032.64 sq. feet

That's 516.32 sq. feet for each side of the roofline, or 1,032.64 sq. feet for just the 2 Story Frame (2s FR/B) section of the home. If we use the auditor website dimensions, I only had 1,028 sq. ft. **for the entire house!**

You'll need to do this measurement conversion ($a^2 + b^2 = c^2$) for each roofline to get a hyper-accurate prediction for potential rainfall catchment.

Now that I've given you the method for determining the *actual* math, you can still use the auditor website to get a "good enough for government work" estimate for a minimum catchment area.

Furthering the example, the rainfall depth for the months of April through September in my area is 22.5 inches. *(I use April to September because that's my growing season and it generally avoids the first and last freeze.)* Now, using the auditor website measurements, all I have to do is multiply using the original formula (Catchment Area x Rainfall Depth x 0.623 Conversion Fraction = Harvested Water (gallons)):

- 1,028 x 22.5 x 0.623 = 14,409.99

In theory, I can harvest almost 14,500 gallons of water in six months! If I were providing exacting math and measurements as previously discussed, and I include the other two rooflines, then that math is as follows:

Auditor Information Conversion Table

Desc	Auditor Dimensions	Actual Dimensions
OP	8' (W) x 14' (L) x 4' (H)	16' (L) x 16.50' (hypotenuse)
2s	26' (W) x 26' (L) x 12' (H)	28' (L) x 18.44' (hypotenuse)
1s	12' (W) x 20' (L) x 12' (H)	13' (L) x 17.70' (hypotenuse)

* Please note that the height measurements were not in the auditor diagram but are needed for the conversion.

Actual Dimension Math

OP:	16 (L) x 16.5 (hypotenuse) = 264 sq. ft
2s:	28 (L) x 18.44 (hypotenuse) = 516.32 x 2 = 1,032.64 sq. ft.
1s:	13 (L) x 17.70 (hypotenuse) = 230.10 x 2 = 460.2 sq. ft.
Total Sq. Ft. Calc.:	264 + 1032.64 + 460.2 = 1756.84 sq. ft.
Rainfall Collection Calc.:	1756.84 x 22.5 x 0.623 = **24,626.5 gallons**

Now, let's have realty set in. I obviously can't store that much as I only have six 50-gallon containers. Plus, my garden isn't that big and I don't need that much water during ANY given growing season. However, you can quickly see how fast it all adds up.

During an interview I gave on the Prepper Podcast with Ken Jensen, we had a lengthy discussion regarding water harvesting, how it worked, and collection sources. During that discussion, I laid out my premise regarding roof collection. It made sense. The house doesn't move and the math is always the same. I had only heard or conceived of collecting rainwater from my roof. Ken postulated that you could place a gutter at the bottom of an exterior wall as well since rain falls at an angle, not straight down. In the end, I had to agree. This was a viable option too.

Here are some references that'll help start building your knowledge base when it comes to water harvesting and purification:

- Essential Rainwater Harvesting: A Guide to Home-Scale System Design by Rob Avis P. Eng and Michelle Avis P. Eng
- Harvesting H2O by Nicholas Hyde
- Rainwater Harvesting and Use: Understanding the Basics of Rainwater Harvesting by Anthony Zagelow
- The New Create an Oasis with Greywater 6th Ed by Art Ludwig
- Water Purification by Will Jameson

Cistern

Having a cistern is an excellent way to store large quantities of water for future use. Typically, cisterns that are filled by a well are underground as well so the water is not contaminated. You could fill a cistern via rainwater just as easily but that water would still need to be boiled for food prep and drinking water. In order for a cistern to be an option for drinking water when you don't have power, meaning water that doesn't need to be boiled, you need two things:

1. A well or natural spring, and;
2. Elevation (gradient from well to cistern to house) or a hand pump (syphon)

As I note later on in the *Electricity,* and again in the *Laundry and Hygiene* sections of this chapter, having a well has some distinct disadvantages during a power outage. However, if you happen to be on well water it doesn't mean that you're completely out of luck in a prolonged power outage. There are some definite advantages as well. Having an underground cistern is one of them.

The following URL will give you some idea as to the wide variety that is available for prefab cisterns.

- https://www.watercache.com/portfolio/rainwater-cisterns-tanks

There are many proponents for cisterns, especially in rural areas, where the criteria noted above (gradient) is met. However, what they espouse is a concrete cistern filled continuously by the well while power is readily available. Concrete cisterns are generally less expensive and fail less frequently than plastic containers and bladders.

During construction/installation of a cistern, an overflow is installed. To maximize your water resources, this overflow should head to a series of water features installed on the property like ponds (fish, stock, man-made, etc.). To keep the cistern viable in a power outage, a solar pump kit is installed. Gravity does the rest and there's no need to boil.

Food

In *Chapter 3 - Minor Disruptions*, we covered some basic short-term shelf-life items that are available in your grocery store. Telling you to just double or quadruple everything isn't very cost effective. To solve this, let's discuss and review some information on items that are available in bulk at your local big box store.

Bulk Food Purchases

The big box stores are really good places for the bulk purchases of things like oils, sugar, flour, rice, beans, spices, etc. Be warned though. You need to have a game plan for these purchases before you buy them. Restaurant owners don't have an issue because they are planning to cook that 50-pound (50#) bag of rice inside of a week. Same for the homesteader, self-sufficiency, and off grid folks except they plan to divvy up all 50# into food grade 5-gallon buckets using the dry ice method, oxygen absorbers, or a vacuum sealer.

Storage and future use is the mindset you need when buying in bulk. Additional costs savings can be found if you were to combine your purchase dollars with other families that are preparing as well and buying by the case lot.

Big box stores like Sam's and Costco are good places to find large #10 sized cans of certain items as well. That being said, one of the things I like to purchase here are hygiene products and pasta. It's an odd combination, I know. My recommendation is for you to go to one of these stores with no agenda and just walk around.

I did that one time while I was doing some research. I literally went aisle by aisle with a calculator and a notepad. Some of those notes I've included in the *Bulk Cost List* tables.

Look at the price per ounce for items I found in a big box store that are on our grocery store list. If you were to procure some food grade barrels, you wouldn't have to worry, at least for a time, if we happen to enter a major disruption period. For ease of use, I rounded up the cost of items to the whole dollar.

Bulk Cost List - Flour

Size	Item	Cost	Price Per Ounce
10#	All Purpose Flour	$5	$0.03
25#	All Purpose Flour	$7	$0.02
25#	Bread Flour	$7	$0.02

Bulk Cost List - Oil

Size	Item	Cost	Price Per Fluid Ounce
1.25G	Canola Oil	$7	$0.04
1.25G	Vegetable Oil	$8	$0.05
2.5G	Corn Oil	$18	$0.05
3.15G	Olive Oil	$16	$0.04
4.5G	Clear Frying Oil	$17	$0.03
4.5G	Peanut Oil	$35	$0.06
4.5G	Soy/Vegetable Oil	$16	$0.03

Bulk Cost List - Rice

Size	Item	Cost	Price Per Ounce
10#	Long Grain Rice	$5	$0.03
20#	Basmati Rice	$20	$0.06
20#	Sona Masoori Rice	$15	$0.04
25#	Jasmine Rice	$18	$0.05
25#	Long Grain Rice	$9	$0.02
50#	Jasmine Rice	$32	$0.04
50#	Long Grain Rice	$17	$0.02

Bulk Cost List - Sugar

Size	Item	Cost	Price Per Ounce
1.2#	Splenda	$11	$0.57
7#	Brown Sugar	$5	$0.04
7#	Powdered Sugar	$5	$0.04
10#	Sugar	$5	$0.03
25#	Sugar	$12	$0.03

Outside of the item types noted in the *Bulk Cost List* tables, I also found 4# of salt (used for flavoring and curing) for $2 ($0.03 per ounce) and 3# of flaxseed (grain) for $7 ($0.15 per ounce). There were no other sizes available for either AND there were no other grains available.

Pre-Packaged Food Options

Incorporating some pre-packaged food options can help in a minor disruption but long-term storage food, generally speaking, is geared more toward moderate and major disruptions.

For the sake of peace of mind, many people will invest in some degree of a one to three month supply of pre-packaged supplies. However, due to cost, they usually only purchase this supply for one person in their family with the intention of splitting the meals up to feed the family for a week to a month. That being said, you can get all manner of 1-week, 1-month, 3-month, 6-month, and 1-year bulk food packages as an emergency cache from places like:

- Food Insurance
- Mountain House
- My Patriot Supply
- Prepare Wise
- Survival Supply
- Valley Food Storage
- Wise

I've provided those names/references because they are the bigger names in the industry. You should do your own research and decide what best suits you, your family, your tastes, dietary restrictions, and your budget when it comes to ultra-long term food storage supplies, regardless of the duration you are preparing for.

You have several options when it comes to not only the quantity but also the type. By that I mean, the weekly, monthly, or yearly supply can arrive as prepackaged meals, individual ingredients, freeze dried, or boxes upon boxes of #10 size cans. For clarity, a #10 sized can is similar to the can size delivered to restaurants. These are BIG honking cans!

The most likely food storage solution, based solely on the financial, is going to be a mix of short-term family staples, self-canning bulk purchases in food grade buckets, canning your own, or locally grown, produce, and pre-packaged food with 20+ year shelf life from reliable sources.

For my family, we utilize *My Patriot Supply*. I didn't come to this conclusion or recommendation lightly. I simply did what you should do. That is to say, I did my research. I taste tested, price shopped, and read labels until I was blue in the face. This supplier had a wide variety of mostly freeze dried goods, but some were meals and some were individual ingredient items and sides. I prefer freeze-dried because of one major factor: weight. Fear not though, we will be discussing the weight of it all later on.

Now don't get me wrong, there are pros and cons for each to be sure. For example, Food Insurance also sells the supplies needed to package your own food (specifically rice and grain) in buckets and Mylar pouches. However, you can find food grade buckets and pouches elsewhere for cheaper. That being said, I am a huge anti-GMO proponent, therefore, *My Patriot Supply* is what I settled on because, in my opinion, they are using higher quality non-GMO ingredients, guarantee a 25-year shelf life, AND I can get my heirloom seeds there as well. Full disclosure, no, I don't work for them and I am not a paid endorser. They've always just been a good supplier for my needs.

When you are considering pre-package food as part of your short and long-term solution, you must consider several notable concepts. These are:

- Cost
- Calories
- Servings
- Portability

Servings per Person

When viewing a supplier's options for what they offer from one-week to one-year, they are pretty up front with their costs. Calories aren't always easily found though and most of the time it requires you to do the math based off any nutritional information they provide. That being said, another oddity I noticed while doing this research was that their designated allocation (three, six, or 12-month supply, etc.) didn't always align with basic math for the number of servings.

Meaning, even though the manufacturer's math is based off one-person for the number of servings it doesn't always align with three meals per day multiplied by the designated number of days. The basic math for serving count for one person should be:

- One Week Supply:
  - 1 person x 3 meals per day x 7 days = **21 meals**
- Two Week Supply
  - 1 person x 3 meals per days x 14 days = **42 meals**
- 1-Month Supply:
  - 1 person x 3 meals per day x 30 days = **90 meals**
- 3-Month Supply:
  - 1 person x 3 meals per day x 90 days = **270 meals**
- 6-Month Supply:
  - 1 person x 3 meals per days x 180 days = **540 meals**
- 12-Month Supply:
  - 1 person x 3 meals per day x 365 days = **1095 meals**

You should be able to do your own math quickly when it comes to the number of servings you need for your family when purchasing these pre-package emergency kits.

Simply take the number of meals per day you are trying to fulfill (1, 2, or 3) and multiple it by the number of people you are trying to feed, and then multiply that by the number of days you are trying to cover. For a minor disturbance, that is 7 days at a maximum, moderate is thirty days maximum, and major is thirty days or more minimum (you decide the duration potential).

For convenience, here's the math for our nuclear family of four:

- One Week Supply:
  - 4 people x 3 meals per day x 7 days = **84 meals**
- Two Week Supply
  - 4 people x 3 meals per days x 14 days = **168 meals**
- 1-Month Supply:
  - 4 people x 3 meals per day x 30 days = **360 meals**
- 3-Month Supply:
  - 4 people x 3 meals per day x 90 days = **1080 meals**
- 6-Month Supply:
  - 4 people x 3 meals per days x 180 days = **2160 meals**
- 12-Month Supply:
  - 4 people x 3 meals per day x 365 days = **4380 meals**

I'm sharing the math because it is vitally important that you get the correct amount of food and that you get what you paid for. You do not want to be the one that has to tell your family/group that your one-year supply of food is going to run out in nine or ten months.

Even when purchasing these kits, depending on the duration of the event, you'll definitely want to supplement this reserve. This can be done through gardening, foraging, hunting/trapping, and fishing. In so doing, you'll be able to stretch this supply. These concepts will be covered more in depth in later chapters.

Pre-Packaged Cost List

Now that you know how many servings per person you are *supposed* to get in this kits, here's what I found when I looked at just three of the suppliers. I highly recommend you do your own comparisons as the information and pricing tends to change with demand and circumstance (2020 has strained all sources, for example).

Distributor – Food Insurance (5-year shelf life)

1-Wk	2-Wk	1-Mth	3-Mth	6-Mth	1-Yr
n/a	n/a	$600	$1800	$3600	$7100
		48 serv	144 serv	288 serv	576 serv

Distributor – Mountain House (30-year shelf life)

1-Wk	2-Wk	1-Mth	3-Mth	6-Mth	1-Yr
n/a	$330	$625	$1835	$3700	$7400
	80 serv	200 serv	600 serv	1200 serv	1800 serv
	1436 cal				

Distributor – My Patriot Supply (25-year shelf life)

1-Wk	2-Wk	1-Mth	3-Mth	6-Mth	1-Yr
$74	$157	$297	$797	$1497	$2897
42 serv	92 serv	284 serv	852 serv	1704 serv	3408 serv
1500 cal	1500 cal	2000 cal	2000 cal	2000 cal	2000 cal

Gardening

Significant cost savings can be found in growing and canning your own food. In addition to cost savings, there are major health benefits, both physical and mental. Having purchased foodstuffs on hand for a minor disruption will get you through in a pinch, but when you transition into a moderate disruption, you need to start thinking more about, and factoring in, cost. Therefore, supplementing what you've bought with food you've grown and/or canned yourself is always a good idea. This helps to reduce your cost burden and gets you moving around outside. Exercise is good, people.

The key to gardening is planning. You need to know:

- What can and cannot grow well in your area
- The composition of your soil
- The amount of direct sunlight
- The average rainfall in your area

Track the sun and recognize not only how much sunlight the garden location would receive in a day, but also if there are any obstructions that could block sunlight. Think of a garden the same way you would approach the installation of solar panels. You are going to want at least eight solid hours of sunlight for a robust garden. However, too much sunlight can be just as bad. If this is your issue and you notice the plants are having difficulty then you'll need to install some shade screen to give the plants a little break during the hottest part of the day.

Lastly, if your area is known for heavy downpours or higher than normal amounts of rainfall, you might want to consider building mounds (hugelkultur) or raised beds. You'll also need to ensure good/better drainage. Working in this manner allows the plants to get the water they need without being flooded repeatedly during the growing season. The downside to this is they'll require more water during prolonged periods when the rain isn't falling as often.

So, can you grow food?

Well, before you get too far, you need to know your Cold (Plant) Hardiness Zone. Review the USDA Cold Hardiness Zone map using the following URL:

- https://planthardiness.ars.usda.gov/PHZMWeb/Default.aspx

Once the zone is known, come up with a list of a half dozen plants that are compatible with your climate (zone) that you'd like to try to grow. Get the hang of playing in the dirt, mending soil, etc.

Understanding your soil, its composition, nutrient levels, etc. is vitally important. This will determine how well or how poorly your garden performs. Learn everything you can about what your soil needs to return it to a good, or enhance its, pH level.

To get you started, the first two questions you need to answer are:

1. Does your soil have too much nitrogen, phosphorous, or potassium, or not enough?
2. How do I mend the soil to adjust the pH?

To adjust a soil's pH, most gardeners will use a combination of soil amendments and fertilizer.

A soil amendment is any material added to a soil to improve its physical properties, such as water retention, permeability, water infiltration, drainage, aeration, and structure. The goal is to provide a better environment for roots. To do its work, an amendment must be thoroughly mixed into the soil.

Many types of soil amendments exist, each with a different role. Some of the most common types include:

- Organic Matter
  - Improves water and nutrient retention and increases the activity of beneficial microorganisms.
- Lime
  - A source of calcium that raises the soil pH.
- Elemental Sulfur
  - Slow acting amendment that lowers the soil pH.
- Ammonium Sulfate
  - Fast-acting and high in nitrogen and lowers the soil pH more quickly than elemental sulfur.
- Gypsum
  - Helps modify soil without any significant change to soil pH. This amendment increases water penetration, loosens compacted clay soils and promotes easier root penetration.

As for fertilizer, all bags have labels that contain three bold numbers. The first number is the amount of nitrogen (N), the second number is the amount of phosphate (P2O5) and the third number is the amount of potash (K2O). These three numbers represent the primary nutrients (nitrogen (N) – phosphorus (P) – potassium (K)).

To get you started, I recommend the following resources if you have the space for an in-ground garden:

- The Backyard Homestead by Storey Publishing, edited by Carleen Madigan
- The Grow Your Own Food Handbook by Monte Burch
- Mini Farming: Self Sufficiency on a 1/4 Acre by Brett L. Markham
- Raised Bed Vegetable Gardening With Hugelkultur by James Paris
- Square Foot Gardening by Mel Bartholomew

If you are convinced that your sole purpose on Earth is to kill plants, then perhaps start by trying to grow one, or a few, plants in a container.

Here are some resources for container and urban gardening, or if space is limited:

- Container Gardening for Beginners by Jordan Bryce
- Container Gardening Month by Month by Gloria Daniels
- Field Guide to Urban Gardening by Kevin Espiritu
- The Vegetable Gardener's Container Bible by Edward C. Smith

A word of caution with container gardening, and where many budding gardeners go wrong, is not recognizing that as you water, you are effectively washing nutrients out of the container. These nutrients need to be replenished frequently or your soil won't do its job.

Homemade Soil Test

In most areas around the United States, the goal, or ideal, soil for your garden is a soil composition referred to as 'loam.' Loam is a composite made up of 40% sand, 40% silt, and 20% clay. You can do your own quick check of the soil composition in your garden area before each growing season in as little as a few hours. All you need is:

- Quart size Mason jar
- 2-3 trowels worth of garden soil
- Water

To perform this test, fill the quart size Mason jar half-full with garden soil. You not looking for a core sample of any prescribed depth. Just take a couple trowels worth of dirt from a random location in your garden. If you have raised beds, maybe consider separate samples in separate Mason jars so you can quickly see what each bed may need.

Once the dirt is in the jar, fill the jar to within an inch of the top with water. Now cap the jar(s) and shake vigorously for a couple minutes. If there are multiple samples, you need to label the jars accordingly. Set the jars aside for a few hours and let things settle out.

Once the soil settles, you will be able to see different layers of varying soil types, one on top of the other.

Any sand and rocks will be on the bottom. Above the sand is the silt layer. At the top of the sediment is the clay. If there is any organic material present, it will be floating near the top of the jar.

If you have loamy soil, you'll have equal parts of sand and silt. Your clay layer will be half as thick as the individual sand and silt layers. Here's a breakdown of what you might see in your Mason jar for the Homemade Soil Test:

- Loam – 40% sand, 40% silt, 20% clay
- Sandy Loam – 65% sand, 20% silt, 15% clay
- Silty Loam –20% sand, 65% silt, 15% clay;
- Silty Clay Loam – 10% sand, 60% silt, 30% clay

Once you determine if your soil is loam, silty clay loam, sandy loam, or silty loam you can make adjustments accordingly. Here's what you need to do for each soil composition type:

<u>Sandy Loam Soil</u>: Amend sandy loam soil by tilling in compost or manure. Be careful though. Compost and manure contain high levels of salt, which damages plants. If you have a high salt content, use only plant based compost.

<u>Silty Loam Soil</u>: Amend silty loam soil by tilling in 1" Coco Peat (aka coconut husk for aeration), 2" of Perlite (volcanic glass used for drainage), and 4" of compost (water retention).

<u>Silty Clay Loam Soil</u>: Amend silty clay loam soil by tilling in 1" Coco Peat (aeration), 4" of Perlite (drainage), and 6" of compost (water retention).

It's easy enough to see what the composition of your soil is with this Mason jar test. However, to determine the chemical make-up of your soil, you'll need to collect a sample, *after* you have amended it to get it as close to loam as possible, and send it in for testing. Use the following URL to determine where to send your soil samples in your state: [Full URL: https://gardeningproductsreview.com/state-by-state-list-soil-testing-labs-cooperative-extension-offices/]

Tools

Depending on the size of the garden, you'll need a couple things. At a minimum, you'll need:

- Fencing material
- Garden Trowel
- Garden Rake (hard)
- Gloves
- Hoe
- Hose (solid and soaker)
- Leaf Rake
- Posts (t-posts or 4x4)
- Round Nosed Shovel
- Square Nosed Shovel
- Tiller (optional)
- Tractor (disc, plow, and/or rake attachments (optional))

If you need to remove bushes, shrubs, or trees to get the garden where you want it, then you'll likely need:

- Axe
- Chain saw
- Pickaxe
- Saw sharpening tools (electric, file, bar mounted stone grinder)
- Spare chain saw chain (multiple)
- Splitting Maul (for firewood afterward)
- Wedges (for firewood afterward)

As an example, my smallest family garden measures about 16x14, or ~ 225 square feet. I have utilized raised beds with decorative rock walkways so not all of that square footage is tilled. The rock also serves to retain heat that dissipates in the evening hours.

To make things easier, I purchased a tilling attachment for my weed-eater. I highly recommend a tiller when you're installing your garden. It also comes in handy when you are working the soil each year in preparation for the next growing season.

Fire

Beyond what was already noted for supplies regarding 'Fire' in Chapter 3, if you are planning on a moderate or major disruption, you'll need to learn what are called 'primitive skills' when it comes to starting and maintaining fire. This means researching different methods and then attempting to use those methods to start a fire. Think of the TV series *Survivor* or the movie *Castaway*. Primitive fire making skills are/were showcased prominently in each.

Perhaps you recognize the method when you see it, but don't know the name. That's easy enough to address with a basic web search. Some of the terms you might want to research when it comes to primitive fire making methods are:

- Bow Drill
- Fire Plough (used on *Castaway*)
- Flint and Steel (used on *Survivor*)
- Friction Drill (two-man)
- Hand Drill

Here's an article that helps explain these primitive skills and more [Full URL: https://www.instructables.com/id/7-Methods-of-Primitive-Fire-Starting/].

Additionally, you can purchase a traditional flint and steel or a magnesium block flint and starter online for cheap ($6-$20 on Amazon depending on what you prefer). For me, I have several types but the two I have found the most success with are:

- Uberleben Zunden Fire Starter (3/8") ($18)
- Magnesium Block Fire Starter w/ Flint and Striker ($6)*

* Because the magnesium will eventually be exhausted, I tend to collect this type of fire starter. I'm well on my way to filling a 5-gallon bucket. I do this because, like I said, the magnesium is a consumable but they are also small, lightweight, compact, and an inexpensive barter item.

When it comes to strictly primitive fire starting, because the two options I just listed are exhaustible resources, I prefer the bow drill if I'm by myself and the friction drill if someone is with me. The reason these two methods are preferred is simple. It preserves the hands and allows physics and chemistry to do the work.

Here are some references that'll help start building your fire making knowledge base:

- Fire Skills - 50 Methods for Starting Fires Without Matches by David Aman
- Fire Making: The Forgotten Art of Conjuring Flame with Spark, Tinder, and Skill by Daniel Hume
- Guide to Making Fire without Matches: Tips, Tactics, and Techniques for Starting a Fire in Any Situation by Christopher Nyerges and Al Cornell

Shelter

Your family's shelter needs can become very complicated in a moderate disruption if you are not still in your home. Camping for a weekend can be fun and all, but at some point, you start yearning for something a little more stable or permanent.

If available, you could attempt to construct a small structure using reclaimed materials from your uninhabitable home. It would likely be primitive and resemble a downtown homeless shanty or something from the pioneer days, but it would be functional and keep everyone out of the elements. If you were some place remote, I would definitely recommend that you do some research on primitive dwellings that allow you to utilize resources in your immediate vicinity.

These dwellings could be structures like:

- Earthen Cave
- Hut
- Lean To
- Log Cabin
- Natural Cave
- Rock House
- Teepee
- Wikiup
- Yurt/Ger

What you construct is entirely up to you given your knowledge base, time constraints, physical abilities, material availability, etc. Use this time *before* a disruption to *expand* your knowledge base. Go out into the woods nearby and see what exactly is available to you in terms of location and materials. When you return, perform an assessment of your tools and address any shortcomings you identify.

Whatever you build should address some or all of the following:

- Large enough for the entire family
- Provide a windbreak
- Remove the elements from the equation
- Retain Heat
- Security from natural predators

Pay attention to the landscape. Avoid spots that show signs where excessive runoff typically occurs or where water collects in pools. Taking a walk in the area you are contemplating immediately after a storm is extremely beneficial for this.

Here are some references and links to some articles that might help expand your knowledge base.

- Shelters, Shacks, and Shanties: A Guide to Building Shelters in the Wilderness by Daniel Carter Beard
- The Lean To and Its Variants Used in Survival and Bush Bough Beds by Mors Kochanski
- https://www.outdoorlife.com/survival-shelters-15-best-designs-wilderness-shelters/
- https://survivalskills.guide/long-term-survival-shelters-alone/

In a perfect world, you wouldn't need any of this information and your home would still be inhabitable. However, the world isn't perfect and sometimes things happen that are beyond our control. That being said, there is absolutely no reason why you couldn't construct a back-up site on your property and maintain it long before you ever need it.

If primitive skills, or constructing something from literally nothing, isn't something that's in your wheelhouse, you could always go with a canvas tent similar to ones the pioneers utilized as they expanded the country westward. These are quite nice and I've used several on multi-week hunting trips.

Canvas tents can take a beating, are easy to repair, handle wood burning stoves, and comfortably sleep several grown men, but they are heavy and expensive. A basic web search for the term 'canvas tent' reveals a variety of sizes and price points. Based on your needs, expect to spend anywhere from $400-$1000 if you go this route.

***

Now that we've taken a deeper dive in to the four topics comprising the Basics, let's dig in to some of the topics I've mentioned previously. These topics include electricity, fuel, laundry & hygiene, and location & security.

***

Electricity

The lack of electricity in a minor disruption is, more or less, an annoyance. Not having electricity for, up to, a month is a huge hurdle to overcome. Fear not though, you have options.

Gas Powered Generator

The least expensive and most portable option is a gas-powered generator. Having one of these is less expensive on many fronts. First is the cost of the generator itself. Depending on the wattage generated, based on your needs, prices for a gas powered generator range from $300-$1,200. Popular procurement sites include:

- Amazon
- Harbor Freight
- Home Depot
- Lowe's
- Northern Tool
- Tractor Supply
- Walmart/Sam's Club/Costco

Your electrical needs will be solely based on what you need to keep fed with electricity. I would avoid trying to power TV's and computers and focus more along the lines of refrigerators, freezers, sump pumps, and well pumps. If family members require medical devices, then you definitely need a backup plan and should plan for that electrical need as well.

Here are some examples of household items that you might power with a gas-powered generator during a minor or moderate disruption (wattage numbers listed are estimates, check your appliances/devices for accurate wattage numbers):

Device	Running Watts	Starting Watts
Box Fan (20")	200	0
Electric Water Heater	4500	0
Freezer (stand-alone)	700	2200
Refrigerator w/ Freezer	700	2200
Space Heater	1800	0
Sump Pump (1/2 hp)	1050	2200
Water Well Pump (1/3 hp)	1000	2000
Window A/C Unit (10k BTU)	1200	3600

All of the items noted above can be run via extension cord from the generator itself. However, if you are going to try to hook the generator directly to your homes electrical panel, I suggest three things.

1. Purchase an inverter*
2. Purchase a transfer switch
3. Hire a professional

* Installing an inverter and a transfer switch are necessary if you want to hook the generator up to your panel and run a few select circuits. That being said, some generators come with an inverter built in. A transfer switch is essential when using a power inverter that is connected to an AC source so that the inverter is not "backfed" when power is applied to the same line. By hiring a professional, they'll be able to help you size the generator and determine whether you need the inverter.

If your aim is to power the furnace and A/C unit, then a portable gas-powered generator is likely not a viable option. However, if you want to power the circuit(s) that has/have the refrigerator, stand-alone freezer, sump pump, and a well pump, then this option might work for you. The key to this solution is to size the generator appropriately. If the generator doesn't produce enough wattage, you'll have brownouts, trip a circuit breaker on the generator, and/or damage the generator.

Additional items to be mindful of when purchasing a portable gas-powered generator are:

- Fuel consumption
- Noise signature

The more electricity that you are pulling from the generator the faster it will burn through the fuel in its tank. On average, if you are running 2-3 extension cords to power the refrigerator, freezer, and sump pump, for example, you'll likely need to fill the tank at least twice a day.

Honda makes a 2200-watt generator (model EU2200i) that retails for about $1,000 while a similar wattage generator by Rainier (model R2200i) retails for about $470. Both hold a little over a gallon of fuel, have a built in inverter, and both claim to be conversation quiet (~52 dBA). The Honda model, though, allows identical units to be run in parallel with an optional cable, which effectively doubles the wattage output to 4,400 watts and doubles the number of available outlets. Both of these models only have two 3-prong outlets and neither of these models provides a 4-prong outlet.

If you require more wattage from the outset, consider looking at the Generac Portable Generator (10,000 watt) which retails on the Northern Tool website for $1,000, or the Westinghouse (7,500 watt) on Amazon for $925, or the Predator (9,000 watt) on the Harbor Freight website for $600. All three of these models have much larger fuel tanks, come with four 3-prong outs, one 4-prong outlet, but they run in the 72 dBA range. This is not a quiet solution.

Do yourself a favor and choose a generator that will provide you with the ability to power the most appliances and is as fuel efficient and quiet as possible. You don't want to have hear the generator-running day in and day out. A noisy generator signature is more than just annoying though. It can also make you a target for thieves when no one is around.

Lastly, if you are experiencing a moderate disruption of services, your ability to acquire more fuel may be hampered. One of three things will happen at this point.

You will either:

- Store copious amounts of fuel and keep it stabilized with a product called Sta-Bil
- Burn precious fuel reserves in your vehicle in search of more fuel for the generator, or
- Run out of fuel and lose most of your refrigerated and frozen food stuffs (perishable items) that haven't been consumed yet.

Since math is a central theme when it comes to preparedness planning, here's what you might need in terms of fuel reserves for small and large generators.

Small Generator

If you go with a smaller generator (lower wattage) that only has a 1-gallon fuel tank, and you follow my two-week recommendation, your math would look something like this:

- 1 gal tank x 2 refills per day = 2 gallons per day x 14 days (2 weeks) = 28 gallons of fuel x $2.50 per gallon = $70.00

In order to fulfill the two-week recommendation, to be safe, you'd need to have six 5-gallon fuel containers stocked and ready to go just for the generator. If the disruption potentially lasts the entire 4-week prescribed duration for a moderate disruption, then you have:

- 1 gal tank x 2 refills per day = 2 gallons per day x 30 days (1 month) = 60 gallons of fuel x $2.50 per gallon = $150.00

Things just got out of hand very quickly.

To solve this storage problem, I would recommend the following:

- Store as many 5-gallon cans as your capacity dictates/allows
- If you know the storm is coming, go and top off your vehicle(s) fuel tank(s)
- Ration the fuel and only run the generator when necessary
- Purchase a fuel syphon kit ($4 on Harbor Freight/$8 on Amazon)

By factoring in the fuel residing in your vehicle(s), you could conceivably outlast a moderate disruption of services. Each vehicles fuel tank holds, on average, 15-25 gallons of fuel that could be utilized in an emergency. The general rule of thumb is the smaller the vehicle, the smaller the fuel tank. Fuel-efficient cars have only 10-15 gallon tanks.

If you haven't figured it by now, the key to preparedness planning is resourcefulness. Look around and use what you have. Think outside the box to solve problems. Creativity in an emergency might just save a life, which could be your own.

Large Generator

Perhaps you are leaning more toward a larger wattage generator. Probably not a bad idea if you need to power more appliances and pumps. Unfortunately, with more wattage comes a bigger fuel tank. The larger generators typically have about a 7.5-gallon fuel tank. You're not going to like this, but here's the math all the same.

- 7.5 gal tank x 2 refills per day = 15 gallons per day x 14 days (2 weeks) = 210 gallons of fuel x $2.50 per gallon = $525.00

If the disruption lasts an entire month, then you have:

- 7.5 gal tank x 2 refills per day = 15 gallons per day x 30 days (1-month) = 450 gallons of fuel x $2.50 per gallon = $1,125.00

At this point, I hope you live somewhere rural because now you are looking at needing a fuel storage tank with a potential to store 500-gallons of fuel or more. Right about now, you're probably thinking a whole house generator doesn't sound like such a bad idea.

Please read *Scenario & Option #2* in the "Laundry – Scenarios & Options" section of this chapter to learn more about trying to power an electric hot water heater via gas generator.

Whole House Generator

Now, if you want to power the bulk of your home, or the entire thing, you'll want to install a whole house generator. This is not an inexpensive, or a quiet, option. Depending of your wattage needs, these generators can run anywhere from $5,000-$10,000 installed and make as much noise as a large portable gas powered model.

As an example, I had an electrician give me a quote for my home. Their recommendation was a 16kW home backup generator with a 16-circuit transfer switch. At the time, I wanted to power the bulk of the house, which encompassed:

- A/C
- Freezer
- Furnace
- Kitchen
  - Dishwasher
  - Lights
  - Outlets
  - Microwave
  - Range*
  - Refrigerator
- Washer (electric) / Dryer (gas)

* The range is gas so I don't have an issue using the stovetop. My issue stems from the ability to turn on the oven. For that, I need the panel on the range to have power to turn on the oven and set the temperature.

Here was their quote:

Item/Task	Cost
16kW Generac w/ Transfer Switch	$4200
Concrete Pad	$325
Elec Material, Battery, Installation	$2000
Plumber Labor and Material	$650
Total	$7175

If I were more selective with the circuits to be powered, I can realize some cost savings by down-sizing the generator and transfer switch to either 13kW ($3,700), 10kW ($3,000), or 7.5kW ($2,000). All of the other costs (concrete, electrical work, and plumbing work) would remain the same, as each of these tasks/items would still need to be handled. The bulk of my initial power needs were associated with the furnace and A/C unit. If you're willing to let those conveniences go, and make some additional sacrifices, you can save a lot of money by downsizing the purchased unit if you choose this option.

Be warned though. The amount of gas (natural gas, propane, or diesel) required to run a whole house generator for a week, let alone for the entire duration of a moderate disruption can provide a great deal of sticker shock when the bill comes.

The only redeeming feature to a whole house generator when it comes to fuel, aside from peace of mind, is that you don't need to store any of it in a gas can.

As far as installation goes, as an example, if your furnace or hot water heater uses propane then the tank (100, 250, 500-gallon, etc.) is already on-site. The plumber would only need to tap into that. If you utilize natural gas for other appliances like I do (furnace, stove/oven, hot water heater, and dryer), then the plumber will tap into the existing line in the house that is being supplied by the city gas feed.

Be warned though. Since we are talking about moderate disruptions of services, there may be a scenario where the pressurization pumps that feed the gas (and/or water) into your home don't have power themselves. If the pumps can't keep the system pressurized, then having a whole house gas fed generator won't do you much good.

Yet another reason to have a back up to your back up.

Solar

If the noisy signature, fuel storage, and fuel cost issues are turning you off generators, you could always go with a solar system to help power the house and/or keep a battery bank charged. Some things to consider if you are contemplating the incorporation of solar into your planning are:

- Do you have an unshaded south facing roof?
- Do you have an unshaded south facing wall?
- Do you have enough land to install an unshaded south facing ground mounted solar rack?

If you can answer 'yes' to any of those three questions, then you might consider incorporating solar into your preparedness planning.

Now comes the bad part, start-up costs.

Installing a solar panel system costs an average of $24,000. Most homeowners pay between $17,000 and $30,000. Expect to pay $2.50 to $3.50 per watt with most systems in the 3kW to 10kW range. These costs don't account for the batteries, which run around $10,000 apiece. Deep cycle marine/golf cart batteries are far cheaper options and can be set up in a series.

Battery Backup

As an example, the Tesla Powerwall costs about $11,500, comes with a 10-yr warranty, and is rated as a 13.5 kW battery. You can read more about this option on their website. [Full URL: https://www.tesla.com/powerwall]. If you use the stored electricity conservatively, the Powerwall option is good for 3-days or so if it is not being recharged by panels. In addition, the Powerwall can initially be charge by the grid and be recharged by your panels. Therefore, your electrical issues could be resolved with this one add-on option.

A competitor to Tesla, named Enphase, has recently come to market with solar panels that use micro inverters behind every panel. They've also developed a battery as well. You can read more about this option on their website. [Full URL: https://enphase.com/en-us/ensemble-technology-enphase-installers] It doesn't have as much capacity as the Powerwall and, because it's a new product, it's a little more expensive.

If you would prefer to save even more money, you could purchase deep cycle batteries to store any collected energy. If you do a basic internet search for the phrase 'deep cycle batteries for off grid', you'll see that these battery types range from $85-$1,000 depending on the voltage (6V to 48V).

Deep cycle batteries require more hands-on maintenance and generally going below 30% of the charge will kill the batteries more quickly, thus requiring replacement. You can read more about the deep cycle battery option in this article on the Realgoods website. [Full URL: https://realgoods.com/off-grid-solar/deep-cycle-batteries] This article will step you through the different types of batteries available as well as the pros, cons, and best uses for each.

Panels

When it comes to solar panels exclusively, meaning, no battery backup, I was provided the following cost breakdown of kilowatt-hours (KWH) if the purchase was financed:

Item/Task	Cost
26 panels generating 543 KWH per month	$42,000
Tax credits	$11,000
Total	$31,000

Most installers/suppliers have financing options if you want to go this route but don't want to pay out of pocket right away. However, I'm not a fan of debt. Nevertheless, this option (solar) has potential and merit, but this type of expenditure needs to be planned and budgeted for. If the purchase were not financed, meaning I paid cash, then the costs would be:

Item/Task	Cost
26 panels generating 543 KWH per month	$37,000
Tax credits	$9,500
Total	$27,500

Now, the reason I am only able to generate 543 KWH per month with 26 installed panels is that my current property only allows for about six hours of direct sunlight on a good day due to trees and the lack of a southern exposure. There's spotty sunlight due to massive trees the rest of the day. However, that amount of generated electricity is nothing to scoff at though. Generating 543 KWH per month consistently means I reduce my grid dependency to half during the summer months when the A/C is running seemingly non-stop and almost covers me for the remaining months, sometimes more than enough.

To see what your energy needs would be for this solution, you need to go online and create an account with your electricity provider (if you don't have a login already) and download your usage. Your energy provider should have records going back many years depending on how long you've used that provider.

The Excel file that I downloaded contained columns for the following information (yours may be slightly different):

- Date
- Days per Billing Period
- Usage (KWH)
- Average KWH's per Day
- Amount Due ($)
- Average Bill per Day

For our purposes here, I just wanted to show you what the inclusion of another energy source could potentially do for a random customer. Therefore, I utilized only the Date and Usage (KWH) columns from the original download. I added in a column for what usage would have looked like if I had a 534 KWH solar system installed (Usage less 534 KWH from Solar) and a column for any energy sold back (Energy (KWH) Sold Back) if the system generated more than I needed in a given month. The green shaded rows are where a 534 KWH system would have satisfied my energy needs for the month and allowed me to sell generated energy back to the provider.

As a result, my analysis for the inclusion of solar would look something like this:

Date	Usage (KWH) without Solar	Usage less 534 KWH from Solar	Energy (KWH) Sold Back
8/11/2020	1,347	813	
7/13/2020	1,320	786	
6/11/2020	1,080	546	
5/12/2020	706	172	
4/13/2020	720	186	
3/12/2020	469	-65	65
2/12/2020	506	-28	28
1/14/2020	795	261	
12/11/2019	645	111	
11/8/2019	472	-62	62
10/10/2019	901	367	
9/11/2019	1,048	514	
8/12/2019	1,056	522	
7/12/2019	1,112	578	
6/12/2019	877	343	
5/13/2019	643	109	
4/11/2019	519	-15	15
3/14/2019	585	51	
2/12/2019	650	116	
1/14/2019	944	410	
12/11/2018	877	343	
11/7/2018	685	151	
10/10/2018	1,074	540	
9/11/2018	1,321	787	
8/10/2018	1,296	762	
7/12/2018	1,388	854	
6/12/2018	1,176	642	
5/10/2018	622	88	
4/11/2018	522	-12	12
3/12/2018	258	-276	276
2/12/2018	930	396	
1/12/2018	800	266	
12/11/2017	697	163	
11/8/2017	599	65	
10/9/2017	309	-225	225
9/11/2017	1,457	923	
Total:	30,406	11,182	683

If my family utilized solar, then we would have used ~ 2/3 less energy over the course of three years (11,182 KWH vs. 30,406 KWH) and we would have been able to give back more than a month's worth of harnessed solar energy (683 KWH). If you're environmentally minded, solar is an excellent way to reduce your carbon footprint.

Going with solar panels and a battery backup definitely removes the 'noise signature' from the equation but adds a lot of initial start-up cost. To get the most bang for your buck, you *must* have the best possible placement for maximum collection and efficiency.

Fuel

In the *Pre-Disruption Planning – Minor* section of Chapter 3, I noted several varieties of fuel that you needed to consider in your preparedness planning. For convenience, I listed:

- Butane
- Charcoal
- Diesel
- Firewood
- Kerosene
- Mixed fuel
- Propane
- Unleaded
- White

In the *Family Planning* section of Chapter 2, I noted several possible reasons for the fuel storage. The reasons for the various types of fuel are as varied as your preparedness goals and equipment supplies allow. What follows is a basic breakdown of the potential types and uses for each fuel type (not all-inclusive):

- Butane
  - Camping stove, meals and boiling water
- Charcoal
  - Grills, meals and boiling water
- Diesel
  - Portable generator, electricity
  - Vehicles, travel
  - Whole house generator, electricity
- Firewood
  - Firepits/grills, meals and boiling water
  - Fireplace, meals and boiling water (potentially) and heat
  - Wood burning stove, meals, boiling water, and heat
  - Wood burning furnace, heat
- Kerosene
  - Heat oil, heat
  - Lanterns, lighting
  - Space heater, heat
- Mixed Fuel
  - Chainsaws, maintenance and tasks
  - Snowblowers, maintenance and tasks
  - Weed Eaters, maintenance and tasks
- Propane (large stationary tank)
  - Furnace, heat
  - Hot water heater, hygiene and laundry
  - Whole house generator, electricity
- Propane (25# LP tank)
  - Grills, meals and boiling water
- Propane (16 oz bottles)
  - Lanterns, lighting
  - Camping stove, meals and boiling water
- Unleaded
  - Portable generator, electricity
  - Vehicles, travel
- White
  - Camping stove, meals and boiling water
  - Lanterns, lighting

That might seem like too many different types of fuel, and it is. The key here is to try to consolidate your fuel choices. What the means is, as you begin your preparedness planning, choose options that allow you to utilize the same type and/or size of fuel container.

For example, I keep and store:

- 25 gallons of unleaded
- 12 Coleman 16 oz. propane bottles
- 6 25# propane tanks (LP)
- 6 bags of charcoal
- 4 gallons of white fuel
- 2 cords of firewood

In essence, I am utilizing three forms of liquid fuel (unleaded, propane, white) and provided two forms of backup fuel (charcoal, firewood). I can use the unleaded fuel in cans (+ the fuel in the cars) to feed the generator. The 25# tanks of propane I keep handy are for my grill, a large double burner stand, gas fire pit, and a patio heater. The fire pit and patio heater are creature comforts that wouldn't necessarily be utilized during a disruption, but the grill and burner would be. The 16 oz. bottles of propane are for single burner camping stoves and lanterns.

In an effort to reduce the number of things littering the yard, I purposefully purchased a grill that had two chambers. On one side is a three-burner gas grill and a side searing grate. The other chamber is a charcoal grill, which can also handle firewood. In addition to a grill, I also procured a multi-function wood burning fire pit. It is multi-function in the sense that I can quickly, and easily, bolt on attachments that turn a decorative fire pit into a camping cook pit with multiple height stands.

Lastly, the white fuel (also known as white gas or Coleman fuel) is needed for a two-burner Coleman camp stove that still works flawlessly and is older than I am.

Your choice of fuel options is solely dependent on your approach to preparedness planning. Now, and I cannot stress this enough, regardless of what devices or implements you go with, you need to actually use them. You must understand how to use your tools before an emergency arrives. You don't need the added stressor of not knowing how to use your equipment on top of that.

Laundry & Hygiene

During the minor disruption, laundry was likely low on the list of priorities. Conversely, hygiene was high. In a moderate disruption, laundry will definitely climb on the list and hygiene will go even higher. Both of these tasks/chores/items will move up the list because I have to assume there is more manual labor given the duration.

For minor and moderate disruptions, you have a few options when it comes to both of these issues.

Laundry – Scenarios and Options

Scenario & Option #1:

You don't have power, but you still have the city water and natural gas feed (or propane tank), AND your hot water heater is gas.

In this scenario, you could conceivably run an extension cord from the generator to the washing machine and do a load of laundry. If you have a gas dryer, you could then move the extension cord from the washer to the dryer to dry the load. If the dryer runs solely on electricity, you'll need a generator that has a 4-prong outlet built in along with this specific 4-prong extension cord. Most portable generators rated 5,000 watt or higher have a 4-prong 125/250V twist-lock outlet.

Gas water heaters don't use electricity as a fuel, and many homeowners assume they will work in a power outage. However, this depends entirely on the type of gas water heater. If your gas water heater uses a continuous gas pilot light, it is likely that your gas water heater will continue to function normally in the event of a power outage. Even gas water heaters with electric pilot lights can continue to work, as they don't necessarily rely on the main panel for electricity.

A note of caution though. If you notice a power cord plugged into the wall and connected to your gas water heater, it's likely it does rely on power from the main and will only supply hot water for a few days in a power outage (the same as an electric tank). If this is the case, and you don't have a generator, be sure to turn off your gas supply in the event of a power outage.

Scenario & Option #2:

You don't have power, you still have a city water feed, but your hot water tank and dryer are electric.

For this scenario, I would run the extension cord to the washer and dryer (4-prong) and avoid messing with the wiring for the hot water heater entirely. Plan to wash clothes using cold water.

The reason I say to avoid the wiring in the hot water heater is that most electric hot water heaters are wired directly into the electrical panel in your home. They are not simply plugged into an outlet.

*** PUBLISHER'S NOTE***

The following information is not meant as instruction. The author and publisher assume no liability for any injuries or damage to person or property that is sustained while attempting to work with electricity. The following is being provided for informational purposes only.

******

Electric water heaters require a 240-volt dedicated circuit, which serves only the water heater and no other appliances or devices. The circuit wiring typically includes a 30-amp double-pole breaker and 10-2 non-metallic (NM) or MC cable. At the water heater, the black circuit wire connects to the black wire lead on the water heater, and the white circuit wire connects to the white wire lead on the water heater.

The white circuit wire should be denoted in some way at the panel and in the hot water heater to indicate that it is a "hot" wire, **not a neutral wire**. Unlike standard 120-volt circuits, a 240-volt circuit carries *live current in both the black and white wires*. The circuit ground wire connects to the green ground screw on the water heater or to the water heater's ground lead, as applicable.

What all of that means is that you'd need to essentially construct your own extension cord out of 10-2 wire. A cord that is capable of being plugged into the generator's 4-prong outlet (male adapter) but has bare wires at the other end to wire directly into the hot water heater. If you go this route, remember to cap the exposed bare wires that you removed from the hot water heater (they are still connected to the panel) with a wire nut and electrical tape for when the power comes back on.

<u>*Scenario & Option #3:*</u>

You don't have power, your well pump doesn't have power, and your hot water heater, washer, and dryer are all electric.

Welcome to life prior to the Industrial Revolution!

If there is no way to power the well pump, then you'll need to go old school and conserve the stored water in the hot water tank for drinking water and meal prep. This means that your free time will likely be spent finding ways to supplement your water needs by collecting or procuring clean water for this task (laundry). This could mean a supply run or rainwater collection. Once that has been accomplished, at this point, you'll need something along the lines of a large galvanized tub or a utility sink. Beyond that, I'd recommend:

- Clothesline and pins
- Detergent/soap
- Hand crank spin dryer/laundry wringer
- Hanging rack
- Washboard

You can find a hand-crank, or foot pedal, spin dryer online for $50.00-$150.00. If you have a generator, you could plug in an electric (110V) spin clothes dryer, those run about $150.00-$250.00. The hand crank laundry wringer costs about $100.00-$200.00. The clothesline, hanging rack, and washboard are inexpensive by comparison at about $25.00 apiece.

See the *Water* section of Chapter 4 for additional information on possible solutions to this scenario.

Hygiene

If your hot water heater is gas and you still have the city water and gas feed, then showering is still an option. However, you might not be so lucky. Now what?

Well, recognizing that the conservation of water is paramount during any disturbance duration, and in order to maintain some level of cleanliness during a disruption, you could utilize one of the following:

- Washcloth and soap
- Solar shower*

* The solar shower option assumes you still have a water feed and it is plentiful but the means to heat it is not.

Most solar showers are about $15.00 and consist of a five-gallon bag with a manual flow valve. These bags are also referred to as camp showers. In essence, you fill the bag with water then let the sun warm the water for a few hours, then hang them and use the warmed water as an extreme slow-flow shower.

There are new freestanding solar showers on the market that allow you to attach a garden hose and fill a built-in 9.5-gallon tank. Once full, the sun will warm the water to approximately 140-degrees. These devices are much pricier at about $150.00.

Location & Security

A moderate disruption, conceivably, can last an entire month. Up until this point, I've presented options and scenarios assuming that the rule of law still exists. I hope that this is the case but hope alone won't fulfill your family's needs during a moderate disruption.

At this point, when it comes to location, I'd like you to look around and ask yourself some questions:

- Would I want to be in this location for an entire month with no services?
- Do I, or can I, trust my neighbors to remain calm in a crisis?
- How safe is my neighborhood, suburb, town, and/or city when the rule of law exists?
- Would I want to be in this location if the rule of law didn't exist?

Now, understand, there are no perfectly safe locations to ride out any disturbance if there is no rule of law when it comes to small towns and large cities. However, some places are better than others. For example, I wouldn't recommend being in a location with millions of residents for any disturbance lasting more than a few days. I would recommend, however, that you seriously consider re-locating to smaller towns away from major cities and the coasts if you are looking to prepare for a moderate or major disruption. When I say 'away from major cities,' I mean at least four hours away by car.

Using the COVid-19 pandemic as an example, it's never been easier to relocate and work remotely assuming you have the capability to work from home. Technology and employer attitudes toward remote work were shoved forward because of the panic, begrudgingly in some case. In some ways, employment and location will no longer be inextricably tied and synonymous. Take this opportunity and use this to your advantage.

In a perfect scenario, you and a group of like-minded families live in a rural location on contiguous parcels of land -or- one of the families (or a couple of the families) is located in this area but plans have been conceived to house group members fleeing more populated areas. The reasons for this relocation are numerous and I've touched on a few of these previously.

A perfect scenario notwithstanding, as an example, in a moderate disruption, if you and yours have planned accordingly and are running a generator but neighbors have not, you'll likely be faced with a different scenario. This scenario is where you are being asked to dole out charity to the un-prepared. Just by having a generator, you're ahead of most people, but that's a blessing and a curse. If the generator is powering lights and illuminating the entire neighborhood, everyone knows where to go to get warm, cool off, store excess food, or plug in an extension cord. They know this because they can hear the generator for blocks and you're lighting up the neighborhood.

To combat these two issues (noise and light), you need to start contemplating ways to exercise noise and light discipline during a disturbance. To reinforce your denial of charity, I would also recommend you become familiar with firearms. Many of these issues can be addressed by gauging friends and neighbors' preparedness planning via discreet conversations to see how they react and what they are willing to disclose. A key term and concept you need to read into and ascribe to is operational security, or OPSEC.

Chapter 5 - Major Disruptions

A major disruption is not anything anyone should ever hope for or want. If an event of this scale befalls the United States, or any country for that matter, many people are going to die. This isn't Chicken Little 'sky is falling' hysterics. This is a fact. The sooner you come to this realization, the sooner you can make sure that you and your family aren't one of the ones being mourned.

Take Venezuela as an example. Currently, this once thriving and wealthy nation is now rife with corruption and gripped with hyperinflation, starvation, disease, and a whole host of other issues mostly stemming from the after effects of a socialist government being installed. At no point, should anyone ever strive for, or romanticize, this form of government, ever.

If we remove national political systems and possibly terrorism from the conversation and focus on weather and natural phenomenon, a little bit of research on the Caribbean gives us a real-world modern example of what to expect. Many islands throughout this region haven't returned to normal life since the hurricanes of 2017 and, as of this writing, it's been over three years. Granted, services were disrupted and the rule of law still exists, but would you want to go through what those islanders have been enduring for more than three years?

Pre-Disruption Planning – Major

Planning for a major disruption literally takes years. Seriously.

A major disruption, by definition, is anything lasting longer than a month. Prior to an event of this magnitude, you need to have everything already in place to aid you and your family. This means planning and preparing years in advance. It will take a significant amount of time to acquire the skills, resources, and knowledge base. A major disruption most likely means that running down the street to the local grocery store is not a viable option AND it entails more than just storing a years' worth of food. You are going to need skills and knowledge to come out of a major disruption. This is especially true if your resources are compromised.

As an example, let's start with food. Having six, nine, or even twelve months' worth of food saved is an excellent place to start. Knowing how to work the dirt, compost, harvest (fruit, vegetables, and seeds), and handle a robust garden would be even better. Planting fruit and nut trees and creating an orchard five to ten years prior to the event would be stellar.

Say you are able to accomplish all of the tasks associated with food storage and seed harvesting. What happens when the house burns down with all of you stored food, seeds, and gear inside?

Well, you are going to need to know two things:

1.   What is a cache and how does it work?
2.   Where can you find fresh food and water out in the wild?

Ever hear the phrase, 'Never store all of your eggs in one basket?' Well, that is the purpose behind a cache. If you have the space, means, and wherewithal, you should divide what you've acquired up into multiple sites so if one site is lost you still have some supplies available to you.

However, if the cache option isn't available to you, you will need to know how to hunt, fish, and trap with multiple weapons, conceal and camouflage, field dress, butcher, and store your kill. You will also need to know how to forage and identify edible plants, roots, and flowers.

All of the skills noted in the previous paragraph take years to acquire. If you have a group, and someone already possesses that skillset, have that person cross-train the other people. This will make knowledge acquisition go a lot faster.

Finally yet importantly, you will need to know how to barter. This is another reason why having a group or community is so important. Mutual aid and assistance is probably the only way anyone is going to successfully handle a major disruption.

A number of the topics covered in this chapter have been discussed previously. However, when it comes to a major disruption, things need to be more robust, possibly serve multiple purposes, and/or function as a back up to your initial plan.

So let's take a look at three of the Basic items (water, food, and fire) in even more detail.

Water

Cultivating water resources before they are needed is critical in a major disruption. Previously, we discussed storing bottled water and rain barrels. In a major disruption, storing cases of water is a non-starter. Rain barrels, however, are still a viable solution as you likely are supplementing your stored food with fresh vegetables, fruits and nuts (hopefully), harvested wild game, etc. Having the rain barrels dedicated to a garden and/or orchard is highly recommended. Having a well or spring with a solar pump kit is better.

With a major disruption, your water options should be renewable. Obviously rain comes and goes, but when it comes, you need to be able to capture as much of it as possible for future use. So how do you do this?

In previous chapters, I noted several things associated with water. Specifically, natural springs, wells, manual/electric pumps, cisterns, and solar panels.

For a major disruption, where you likely won't have power, your best bet would be to invest in renewable energy sources like solar and wind to power pumps and fill an underground cistern from a well. It would be preferable to have the cistern at capacity and incorporated into your plumbing apparatus prior to the event as well.

Outside of a well, you might want to consider other means for water harvesting and storage like ponds or having some form of running water (stream, river, seasonal creek) on or near your property.

Hand Pump

As was mentioned in the *Water* section in Chapter 3, incorporating a hand pump on a shallow well is definitely a viable solution for water in a major disruption. This solution will also make life during a minor and moderate disruption much easier as well. Here are some URL's to give you a little background on this concept:

- https://en.wikipedia.org/wiki/Hand_pump
- https://www.youtube.com/watch?v=It3CvoRxmmE (video)

Wind Pump

A wind pump is exactly what it sounds like. Briefly, a windmill utilizes the wind to power or turn a pump set in a well. It's a good backup but it can be a fickle solution in areas devoid of good or regular winds. Here are some URL's to give you a little background on this concept:

- https://en.wikipedia.org/wiki/Windpump
- https://www.youtube.com/watch?v=cnY2ejP43bA (video)
- https://www.youtube.com/watch?v=8T-6CAsvDgQ (video)

Air Well/Dew Condenser

An air well, or dew condenser, is a condensation tower that, literally, captures water from thin air. This concept has been around for ages and could be utilized to provide some water in just about any climate. I have a friend in west Texas that utilizes this concept on his ranch. Here are some URL's to give you a little background on this concept:

- https://en.wikipedia.org/wiki/Air_well_(condenser)
- https://permies.com/t/airwell
- https://pdfs.semanticscholar.org/b82a/af77fca4b6ebf78923a86c82be4ff1a2ce24.pdf

Land Contouring (Swells & Ponds)

If you happen to own property with even the slightest grade, walk the land during and after a storm to see how and where water is moving across your acreage and/or pooling. Then, using dirt, create swells to better channel the water toward a natural depression or pond (if you have one). If no pond exists, but water pools there for a time after a storm, install a man-made pond and use the excavated dirt from the pond to create the swells. If you have more land available further downhill, install your pond overflow piping or even a decorative spillway so that any excess can fill a second pond utilizing a terraced concept.

A simple shallow trench filled with rock connecting multiple ponds will captured sediment and the area around the spillway can be seeded with native grasses and flowering plants to attract pollinators. The mini ecosystem created by the plants and grasses in the spillway helps to clean and purify the water during transport as well.

If you are serious about preparing for a major disruption, the concept of installing a pond or some form of water feature should seem very attractive for many reasons.

The first reason is available water year round. The second is wildlife. If you have a stable source of water, the wildlife in your area will find and utilize it. This will help you supplement your food reserves and keep you and your family fed if you're able to harvest some of the wildlife. If the water feature is attractive enough and had abundant food either in the feature or in crops nearby, migratory birds like multiple species of duck and goose would frequent the area as they move north and south with the seasons.

Another benefit to land contouring via swells is a gardening concept called hugelkultur. Instead of dumping or moving excavated dirt to create the swells and seed bombing it with grass seed, you could:

- Plant medicinal herbs
- Plant native grasses and plants to attract pollinators
- Sow the swells annually with vegetable seeds

Everything you do to prepare for a major disruption must serve more than one purpose and benefit your family or a group of families in some way.

Open Sources

If none of the previously mentioned options is available to you, then you are going to have to rely on open sources of water. Technically, any water features on your land, like a pond, would be considered an open source too. However, for our purposes here, I am defining open source water as any water source not directly tied to your land by design. This means lakes, streams, creeks, drainage ditches, etc.

If you have to go the route of open source water, I'd highly recommend extensive filtering, boiling, and buckets no larger than 5-gallon. I'd also recommend any wheeled contraption with two or more wheels affixed to it. A mono-wheel wheelbarrow is not a particularly good option due to its propensity to tip over. Moreover, there is carrying capacity to consider.

As I note in the *Portability* section later on, water is 8.34 lbs per gallon. That means that depending on how many buckets you're trying to fill and haul, your load could quickly get into the hundreds of pounds category.

Bucket size	Total Weight
1 gallon	8.34 lbs
2-gallon	16.68 lbs
5-gallon	41.70 lbs

Man has invented many ingenious ways to haul heavy loads over the course of our history. However, the greatest invention, by far, for accomplishing this task, has been the wheeled cart. Do yourself a favor and look at purchasing, or repurposing, a two, three, or four-wheeled garden cart, wheelbarrow (2-wheel), jog stroller, or anything with a max capacity capable of carrying several hundred pounds. Also, look at replacing the factory tires with foam-filled or solid core no-flats.

Water Purification/Filtration

However, even after you've exerted all of that energy to retrieve your water, you still aren't done. All open source water must be filtered and purified. As a result, the ability to stockpile additional means for water filtering and purification outside of t-shirts, towels, and boiling would be extremely beneficial.

Here are some examples of lightweight, semi-cost effective options you can utilize:

- Aquatabs (100 ct - $12.00)
- Gravity Water Filtration Systems ($80.00 - $100.00)
- LifeStraw (1 ct - $15.00)
- Potable Aqua Water Purification Tablets (50 ct - $7.00)
- Potable Aqua PA Plus Tablets (only comes in combo packs with the water purification tablets, used for taste and color only – 50 ct each bottle for $9.00)
- Sawyer MINI Water Filtration System (1 ct - $20.00)

Unfortunately, all of these options contain and/or are consumable commodities. Meaning, you'll need more than one to outlast a major disruption. If you consider these or other water purification and filtration options, you need to pay particular attention to what, exactly, the filter or system is protecting you from. You'll want to find the system, filter, method, and means to remove anything and everything that will either make you violently ill or kill you outright.

Therefore, read everything about the product before you purchase it. You'll want to know if the device removes all or just some of the following:

- Bacteria
- Cholera
- Cryptosporidium
- E. coli
- Giardia
- Heavy Metals
- Pesticides
- Salmonella

There are other contaminates you should be aware of when drinking from open sources so do as much research as possible before the disruption starts. Trial and error and winging it with open source water can kill you and your entire family.

Here are some resources for you to learn more about this topic and read about some field tests:

- https://www.wemjournal.org/action/doSearch?text1=water+disinfection&field1=AllField
- https://www.wemjournal.org/article/S1080-6032(19)30116-4/fulltext

Food

The concept of food has been discussed in each of the preceding chapters. However, long-term food storage solutions can be tricky and require a different skillset than just shopping. You'll need to know how to prepare the items when necessary to get them ready for storage and you'll also need to know how to store them so they last as long as possible.

Long-Term Storage Foods

Long and short-term food supplies that can be found at the grocery store are, and please forgive the term, a dime a dozen. The real question is, of the millions of items I could possibly find in a store, what do I actually need?

Well, first, comfort food is always a welcome distraction especially in dire circumstance. The home front can be stressful all by its lonesome during a disruption. Moreover, comfort foods, or more specifically, comfort *flavors*, have the added benefit of being a morale booster. These foods and flavors generally contain one of the four following ingredients:

1. Salt
2. Sugar – Brown or White
3. Raw Honey
4. Alcohol – Bourbon, Whiskey, Vodka, etc.

It is also important to note that these four items can be stored for over 10 years. The salt can be used to preserve food, as well as add flavoring to dishes. Go easy on it though. With higher sodium comes an increase in water consumption and heart related issues. Sugar, honey, and alcohol can also add flavor, but they are incredibly valuable for barter as well. (We'll discuss bartering later on.) As an added bonus, if stored properly, all four could potentially last indefinitely.

Once you have your comfort flavors taken care of, now you need only concern yourself with the base meal ingredients. I have chosen to separate these base meal ingredients into five categories. Each of these categories serves as the core, or foundation, for all recipes. In addition, again, if stored properly, each can keep for almost a decade.

Base meal ingredients consist of:

- Hard Grain
- Soft Grain
- Beans
- Flours, Mixes, and Pastas
- Oils

Within each of the categories, there are a number of options. After that, it all comes down to preference and taste. What do you, or your family, like to eat?

Additionally, this is where having a group planning together becomes helpful because you can pool your financial resources and purchase items by the case lot and/or directly from the manufacturer. Purchasing from the manufacturer removes the middleman markup too and gives you more realized savings.

Hard Grains:

These ingredients, if stored properly using either the dry ice method, oxygen absorbers, or a vacuum sealer, can remain fresh for nearly 25 years.

- Buckwheat
- Dry Corn
- Kamut
- Hard Red Wheat
- Soft White Wheat
- Millet
- Durum Wheat
- Spelt

Most of these hard grains are available in pre-packaged, pre-sealed buckets in bulk. The bulk items aren't necessarily sold in grocery stores, but if you have coupons or a sale, you can fill a bucket quickly and seal it yourself.

> NOTE: If you're going the hard grain route, find a grinder (grain mill) because some of these can be ground down into flours.

Soft Grains:

Of the soft grains, I've only ever spotted the quinoa and certain varieties of oats in the grocery store. Well, I take that back... I've seen the others on occasion, but they were so cost prohibitive that I just kept on walking. That doesn't mean you can't find them too, but my guess is that, like me, these will most likely have to be bought pre-packaged in bulk storage containers.

- Barley
- Oat Groats
- Quinoa
- Rye

If you seal these using the dry ice method, oxygen absorbers, or a vacuum sealer, the soft grains will last around 8 years.

Beans:

Whether you like it or not, or believe it or not, beans pretty much go with everything. Moreover, they have the added bonus of high amounts of protein. You need this to maintain muscle mass.

- Pinto Beans
- Kidney Beans
- Lentils
- Lima Beans
- Adzuki Beans
- Garbanzo Beans
- Mung Beans
- Black Turtle Beans
- Black-eyed Beans

Just like the soft grains, if you seal these using the dry ice method, oxygen absorbers, or a vacuum sealer, these bean varieties will last around 8 to 10 years.

Flour, Pasta & Rice:

Talk about the ultimate in comfort food! Carbs! Just about every American meal contains one of the three ingredients. Luckily, for me, I do know how to make yeast from fruit and water so I'm set when it comes to leavened bread so I tend to focus on the pasta and rice. Word to the wise, packaged yeast doesn't store well so you had better know how to make your own yeast too. (Yeast making and yeast water will be covered later.)

- White Flour (All Purpose)
- Whole Wheat Flour
- Cornmeal
- Pasta (all varieties)
- White Rice (up to 10 years)
- Whole Grain Rice
- Jasmine Rice

Seal these items up as tight as you can using the dry ice method, oxygen absorbers, or a vacuum sealer, these can last 5 to 8 years.

Oils:

Many recipes call for some form of fat. For our family, we typically only use olive or vegetable oil for cooking.

- Peanut Oil
- Olive Oil
- Vegetable Oil
- Coconut Oil
- Grapeseed Oil

Oils that come in a can seem to last the longest for use. The plastic bottles tend to leak over time... well, the cans will as well, but the plastic bottle variety usually goes first.

NOTE: Coconut oil has one of the longest shelf lives at over 2 years.

In a major disruption, it is highly recommended that you save and render any fat from harvest meat sources. Rendered fat can be used for cooking, as fuel in lanterns, and is a key ingredient when making candles. Review the *Livestock* section for more information on which animal varieties can provide additional fat sources.

Yeast

Yeast naturally occurs in nature on the skin of fruits and vegetables. Well, technically, unless you grew it yourself, a lot of the yeast has been washed off or covered in wax. Therefore, if you want a good yeast, use ingredients that you grew yourself or ingredients that you can trace its sourcing all the back to the grower and ask them if the fruit or vegetable was treated in any way.

As far as making your own yeast is concerned, luckily, there are a variety of options. These are all detailed out in Chapter 2 of another book of mine titled, *Home Remedies, Poultices, Salves, & Tinctures*. That being said, you'll need to be mindful as to your future needs and/or potential uses. Meaning, you might not be distilling your own vodka right now for medicinal tinctures, but it might be a good idea to understand how to start, maintain, and dry your own yeast for the use should the need ever arise.

Typically, you'll need about a 1 C of wet starter (batter like substance) in place of 1 packet of yeast. If you've dried your yeast batter, start out by doubling the amount of yeast called for in the recipe. In most cases, a store bought packet of yeast is 1 oz. so you'll need 2 oz. possibly more. The potency of homemade yeast will be a little different from the store-bought version. Also, use different fruit, vegetable, and herb ingredients when making yeast water. The essence of these ingredients will add new and unique flavors to your baked goods.

For the purposes of this topic, I've included the *Yeast Water* recipe. This is the easiest and least labor intensive of the yeast recipes. The reason being, there are only two ingredients. The rest is just time. I've also included the *Drying Yeast* process should you prefer to use a batter-based yeast.

Yeast Water

Materials:

Wide mouth Mason Jar (w/ lid)
Cheesecloth (optional)

Ingredients:

1-3 C Sliced Fruit/Vegetable/Herb, leave the skin on as this is where the yeast is located (apples, grapes, cucumbers, raisins, etc.)
2-4 C Filtered or Spring Water (not alkaline or chlorinated – this will kill the yeast)

Instructions:

1. Fill a Mason jar 1/3 to 1/2 full with your chosen fruit, vegetable, or herb.
2. Fill the Mason jar 3/4 full with water (filtered or spring, not alkaline or chlorinated city water).
3. Loosely close the jar, or cover with the cheesecloth, and leave in a warm area (in the sun or by a stove) for approximately 3 days or until a good amount of bubbling has begun forming (this is an indication that the yeast is reacting with the carbohydrates in your fruit, veggie, etc.).
4. Once the bubbling action is well underway, you can begin using the yeast water in your baking recipes.

To use in baking, ignore the specified yeast ingredient and quantity noted in the recipe. Simply insert the yeast water in place of both the yeast and water ingredients but use the recipe specified quantity of water (1 Cup, 2 Cups, etc.).

5. Continue with your recipe as usual.

Drying Yeast

Back in the days of westward expansion, one of the challenges faced by many was the making, storing, and transporting of yeast. One of the more widely known stories involving yeast comes from the Book of Exodus when Israelites left Egypt in a hurry. Jews to this day commemorate God's deliverance by abstaining from products with leavening during Passover.

However, if you want to be able to bake bread the instant you arrive (should you find yourself in this situation), then you need to know how to dry and store yeast.

Instructions:

1. Take any of the starters (fruit, potato, sourdough) and spread it very thinly on a cookie sheet or baking stone.
2. Dehydrate the batter as you would anything else.

NOTE: If you live in a hot and dry climate, you may just be able to cover it with a cheesecloth and place in the sun. You can use a food dehydrator (if you have one) or your oven. The following steps utilize an oven.

3. If you are not in a hot and dry climate, set your oven to the lowest temperature possible and place the cookie sheet or baking stone in the oven.
4. Once the yeast is dry (not browned, burnt, and cooked), you can crumble it and store in an airtight container. NOTE: If the temperature is too high and you cook the yeast, you will have killed the active yeast and rendered the entire batch useless.
5. As with anything homemade, it will last longer if placed in the refrigerator or freezer.

Gardening

If there were no electricity, where does one get the necessary nutrients to fend off things like scurvy (vitamin C deficiency), preserving regularity in bowel movements, becoming protein deficient, or a whole host of other maladies during a major disruption? Well, your garden is going to be the primary source of vitamins and minerals that will help keep a wide assortment of ailments at bay during the major disruption. As an example, let's take a quick look at other sources of Vitamin C.

My Cold Hardiness Zone (6a) precludes me from growing any of the usual, recognizable sources of Vitamin C (citrus) without electricity. In order to overcome that, you need to do some research for other sources of this essential vitamin. What I found said that I could find everything I needed in my garden provided I grew the right plants and vegetables that were compatible with my Cold Hardiness Zone.

According to the MyFoodData article I found [Full URL: https://www.myfooddata.com/articles/vitamin-c-foods.php], there are plenty of options that can be grown right in your very own garden to supply Vitamin C. Here are their top ten Vitamin C producers and I've taken the liberty of crossing off the ones that won't grow in my Cold Hardiness Zone:

- ~~Guavas~~
- ~~Kiwifruit~~
- Bell Pepper
- Strawberries
- ~~Oranges~~
- ~~Papaya~~
- Broccoli
- Tomatoes (cooked)
- Snow Peas
- Kale

Six of their top ten can be grown in Zone 6a and all six are vegetables that are easily grown in the garden. To help summarize the article, as there was a ton of fruit and vegetable information, I've constructed this handy table in an effort provide a thorough knowledge base.

Alternative Vitamin C Sources Table

Fruit/ Vegetable	Vitamin C per Cup	% Daily Value per Cup
Guavas	377mg	419%
Kiwifruit	167mg	185%
Bell Peppers	152mg	169%
Strawberries	98mg	108%
Oranges	96mg	106%
Papaya	88mg	98%
Broccoli	81mg	90%
Tomato (cooked)	55mg	61%
Snow Peas	38mg	42%
Kale	23mg	26%

This type of research and planning goes into a well thought out garden plot. The good news is that a lot of this research and planning can be done during the winter when the garden isn't available for planting, tending, or harvesting.

Extending the Growing Season

When it comes to planning for a major disruption, you are going to want to eke out every bit of your growing season. Anything that you can do to start early or plant late and still protect your plants from the chilly nighttime air, wind, or frost means you'll have that much more to make it through the dark days of winter.

You can extend your growing season by using greenhouses, row covers, cold frames, windbreaks, raised beds, and a whole host of other measure.

Here are some articles that'll give you some additional detail and explain some of the ways that you can extend your growing season through a variety of means:

- https://www.gardeners.com/how-to/season-extending-techniques/5063.html]
- https://www.saferbrand.com/articles/extend-growing-season

Tools

When it comes to tools in a major disruption, you need to make sure they don't require anything more than sweat equity to use. Nothing that requires batteries, fuel, or an extension cord are likely going to be available to you. Therefore, you need to look to 19th century, pre-Industrial Revolution, tools. This is the primary reason I stated in *Chapter 4* that you needed to get the garden in place before the disturbance. Installing a garden with powered tools like tillers, tractors, chainsaws, etc. is far easier, less time consuming, and less labor intensive than without.

In addition to the tools noted in the *Gardening* section of Chapter 4, some additional tools you might want to keep an eye out for are:

- Broadfork
- Pitchforks (hay, wide, and narrow tined)
- Saws (one-man hand and two-man crosscut/buck)
- Saw sharpening tools
- Scythe

Now, assuming your fuel (unleaded or diesel) is limited, exhausted or has gone bad you might want to consider tools and implements that revolve around the use of animal labor in the form or horses and cows. Antique yoke, plow, disc, and assorted tilling instruments can be restored back to their 19th century luster and/or fabricated for use by livestock to pull through fields. If you happen to be near Amish country (or similar), you can go and watch them work the land and acquire the knowledge needed to utilize these tools. You could, perhaps, even acquire tools and implements that you know have been maintained and are good working order.

Orchards

Having the ability to incorporate fruit and nut trees into an orchard helps everyone. You, your family, your group/community, and wildlife all can benefit from the planning of this resource. I've added wildlife because fruit and nut trees attract them in droves and will allow you to diversify your food options during a major disruption.

If you think you might want to plan an orchard, I would definitely recommend the Stark Bros website for your research [Full URL: https://www.starkbros.com]. I've found that their website has one of the easiest interfaces for consumers to navigate and there's a wealth of information available about fruit and nut trees as well as a nice variety of berry plants and bushes.

As an example, Stark Bros. published 'Growing Guides' for individual fruits, nuts, and berries as well as a homestead guide for fruit trees. You can find that information here:

- https://www.starkbros.com/growing-guide
- https://www.starkbros.com/growing-guide/article/adding-fruit-to-your-homestead

For all of the information available online, I would still recommend that you procure additional and specific information from local arbors and nurseries.

Fruit Trees

Below is some research on fruit and nut trees that were compatible with my Cold Hardiness Zone. Take some time and do similar research for your own Zone or perhaps the Zone where you think you might want to relocate.

Fruit Trees Table

Fruit Type	Years to Bear	Pollination Type	Mature Size
Apple – Honeycrisp (dwarf)	2-5	Poll Req	8-10'
Apricot – Wilson (dwarf)	2-5	Self Poll	8-10'
Cherry - Blackgold	4-7	Self Poll	15-18'
Fig - Chicago Hardy	1-2	Self Poll	15-25'
Pawpaw - Pennsylvania Golden	5-7	Poll Req	15-25'
Peach - Finger Lakes (dwarf)	2-4	Self Poll	8-10'
Pear - Barlett (dwarf)	4-6	Poll Req	8-10'
Plum - Fellenberg (dwarf)	3-6	Self Poll	8-10'

Take note of the fruit types that state 'Poll Req' (Pollinator Required). This means that you will need to plant more than one of these trees in order for the blossoms to become fruit. Pay close attention to spacing, maturity, and bloom time recommendations offered by the Stark Bros website or your local resource(s). Also, notice that I chose dwarf species when possible. This is for ease of harvesting and tree maintenance.

The Stark Bros website also provides some nutritional information for the raw fruit. One of the things you'll notice right away is that the fruits are high in carbohydrates and low on protein due to their sugar content.

Nut Trees

In order to provide an alternative source of protein, plant some nut trees in your orchard. However, this is easier said than done. Planting nut trees in my Cold Hardiness Zone, like planting fruit trees, automatically creates a limiting factor due to temperature variations. In addition, nut trees add an additional component of sheer size, as they are generally much larger than their fruit bearing brethren. However, there are still plenty of options available to me in my zone.

Nut Trees Table

Nut Type	Years to Bear	Pollination Type	Mature Size
Almond - All-in-One	3-4	Self Poll	12-15'
Chestnut - Auburn Homestead	3-4	Poll Req	30-40'
Hazelnut - Fingerlakes	6-8	Poll Req	18-25'
Pecan - Missouri Hardy	10-20	Poll Req	75-100'
Walnut - Lake English	4-5	Self Poll	30-40'

When selecting you orchard location, pay particular attention to the track of the sun. You'll want the nut trees on the north side of the orchard so they don't shade the fruit trees.

Can you imagine what you'd be able to barter for with a well thought out orchard at your disposal? The possibilities are seemingly endless for bartering if you plan.

Berry Bushes & Vine Fruits

Another way to procure a source of fruit is to plant berry bushes and vine fruits like grapes. As was noted in the *Fruit Trees* section, fruits, or in this case berries, are high in sugar and therefore carbohydrates, but lack a lot of protein. On the plus side, they attract alternative protein food sources in the form of wildlife, particularly birds. Therefore, invest in an air rifle or become adept at using a slingshot and procure many rolls of reusable plastic bird netting if you want to save your harvest. That being said, there are a few things you'll need to know about berry bushes. For example:

- Berries do very well in pots so don't discount patio space in your planning
- Don't place red raspberries within 100'of black raspberries
- Black raspberries and blueberries are high in antioxidants so there's some medicinal properties that can be utilized as well

Here's some nutritional information that'll help provide some clarity as to the benefits of berry bushes and vine fruits in your orchard/garden planning:

Berry and Vined Fruit Table

Berry/Fruit Variety	Cal per C	Carbs per C	Protein per C	Fiber per C	Vit C per C
Black Rasp.	60	15g	1g	8g	32mg
Blackberry	61.9	14.7g	2g	7.6g	30.2mg
Blueberries	84.4	21.4g	1.1g	3.6	14.4mg
Cantaloupe	60.2	52.4g	1.5g	1.6g	65mg
Grapes (grn/red)	104	98.5g	1.1g	1.4g	16.3mg
Honeydew	63.7	16.1g	1.0g	1.4g	31.9mg
Red Rasp.	64	14.7g	1.5g	8g	32.2mg
Strawberries	48.6	11.7g	1g	3g	89.4mg
Watermelon	46.2	11.6g	0.9g	0.6g	12.5mg

Of course, there are dozens of different types of fruit vines and berry bushes. Here's an article that steps through twenty-three berry varieties [Full URL: https://leafyplace.com/types-of-berries/]. Review the article and then research which varieties are compatible with your Cold Hardiness Zone.

The key is to determine what grows in your location and what level of tartness is palatable to you, your family, and/or group/community.

Beyond that, if you have the ability to dehydrate the berries or fruit they become extremely lightweight and make an excellent barter item or as a snack when out hunting or hiking. These options don't account for the pies, jams, jellies, wines, and toppings that can be made from the fruit.

Be careful with the strawberries though. They are super spreaders in the garden plot so they really need to be segregated and walled off with rock or timbers so they don't grow where you don't want them. If anything ever needed to be in a pot or container, it was strawberries.

Here are some resources that will help get you started with vined fruits and berries:

- The Fruit Gardener's Bible: A Complete Guide to Growing Fruits and Nuts in the Home Garden by Lewis Hill & Leonard Perry
- The Holistic Orchard: Tree Fruits and Berries the Biological Way by Michael Phillips
- The Organic Backyard Vineyard: A Step-by-Step Guide to Growing Your Own Grapes by Tom Powers
- https://happydiyhome.com/planting-raspberries/

Root Cellar

While the orchard, vine, and berry crops are maturing, you may want to consider building a root cellar for the storage of abundant garden production. These earthen structures have been used, in one form or another, for millennia to store food without electricity. Think of a root cellar as a cache for food.

Most of the root cellars I've seen have been dug into the side of a hill and a door added afterwards. In some areas, your home's basement can make a suitable root cellar too. If you're in a rocky area, dig down as far as you can, build a structure over that, then cover the structure with any surface or unearthed rocks. If the area isn't rocky, follow the same steps as with rock except cover the structure with dirt and sod.

The most interesting root cellar I've seen was where a couple had buried a shipping cargo container. Prior to covering the container, they place steel I-beams, poured concrete, piled all of the excavated dirt on top, and then seed bombed the dirt mound with medicinal plants.

Recommended Resources:

- Build Your Own Underground Root Cellar by Phyllis Hobson
- Preserving Food without Freezing or Canning by the Gardeners and Farmers of Terre Vivante (read Chapter 1)
- Root Cellaring: Natural Cold Storage of Fruits & Vegetables by Mike and Nancy Bubel
- The Complete Root Cellar Book: Building Plans, Uses and 100 Recipes by Steve Maxwell and Jennifer MacKenzie

Available Food Sources

If a major disruption occurs, you need to know how and where to locate food before the disruption occurs. The term 'food' is a broad term and applies to wildlife, edible items like fruit, nuts, and berries, as well as foraged items like flowers, tubers, and roots.

Wildlife

In order to know what is available to you in terms of wild game, I recommend that you start hiking around the area where you live, or where you plan to relocate. I would go in circuitous routes and consult your state's Department of Natural Resources or Wildlife maps to help guide your walks. Try to verify their data. Talk to hunters too. On your hikes, you are looking for two specific things in addition to the wild game: water sources and food sources for each species you are trying to find. However, I would limit your distances to no more than five miles.

As I noted in the *Land Contouring* section, you can create your own water sources on your own land by implementing water features like a pond or two. You can also entice wildlife with your orchard and specific crops. Utilize this information to ensure you don't have to go far to find fresh meat.

If you cannot find these two items (food and water sources for wildlife) within a reasonable range, you need to find a better area, increase your distance, or consider moving to an area with better natural resources. Be careful though. If you have to increase your range when times are good, you can likely expect that range to be wider when it's not. The wider the range, the more calories are needed to get to your hunting ground and return. I hope that you are successful, but you need to take into account that on the return trip, you'll be burdened with the weight of the kill.

Just about every area (rural, suburban, and urban) has small game that residents of that area are familiar with: pheasant, grouse, rabbits, squirrels, dove, quail, duck, geese, and predators like coyotes, foxes, and badgers.

Review the table below to learn about the typical range for several species of big game:

Species	East/West Range	North/South Range
Alligator	Atlantic/ Central Texas	North Carolina/ Florida Keys
Antelope	Central Nebraska/ Eastern California	Mexican Border/ Southern Canada
Bear (Black)	Appalachian Mtns & Rockies	Gulf Coast/ Central Canada
Bear (Grizzle)	Central Canada/ Pacific Ocean	Northern Rockies/ Arctic
Bison	Spotty pockets/ Plains to Rockies	Northern Texas/ Southern Canada
Boar	Atlantic Ocean/ Pacific Ocean	SE & lower plains Pockets in states
Caribou	Atlantic Ocean/ Pacific Ocean	Canadian border/ Arctic
Coyote	Atlantic Ocean/ Pacific Ocean	Central America/ Arctic
Crocodile	Atlantic/ Gulf of Mexico	Southern Florida
Deer (Mule)	Western Nebraska/ Pacific Ocean	Canadian border/ Mexican border
Deer (White Tail)	Eastern Wyoming/ Atlantic Ocean	Canadian border/ Gulf of Mexico
Elk	Western Nebraska/ Pacific Ocean	Canadian border/ Mexican border
Moose	Atlantic Ocean/ Pacific Ocean	Northern Rockies/ Arctic
Sheep (Big Horn)	Western South Dakota/ Eastern California	Southern Canada/ Northern Mexico
Wolf (Grey)	Atlantic Ocean/ Pacific Ocean	Northern Rockies/ Arctic
Wolf (Red)	Eastern North Carolina	n/a

Additionally, I would highly recommend a fun family activity like taking part in orienteering courses and challenges. Most kids will have learned some basics in the Girl Scouts and Boy Scouts. If you've forgotten those teachings, you can read up on it online just about anywhere with a basic search for terms or phrases like 'orienteering' or 'orienteering near me.' These searches will provide resources like the REI website [Full URL: https://www.rei.com/learn/expert-advice/orienteering-basics.html]. Once you've read up on it, you can take the whole family to nearby courses or register for an event. Online sources like Orienteering USA are a good starting point [Full URL: https://orienteeringusa.org/events/clubs/] to locate groups near you. The lessons and knowledge gained here will help you as you try to locate food and water resources in your area.

Tracking and Trapping

The ability to track and/or trap game is one of the primary reasons our ancestors were able to progress westward after the Louisiana Purchase. There was no way any frontiersmen or wagon train was ever going to be able to carry enough food with them as they journeyed west exploring and establishing new towns and trade routes. To overcome this issue, these brave souls had to find food on their own to supplement what they were able to carry.

Tracking and trapping are skills that take time. You need to learn to decipher the various 'sign' for a variety of animals. For example:

- What does the animals scat (droppings) look like?
- What does the animals track look like? Hoofed, webbed, or paw?
- What does it look like where the animals have bedded down?
- Does the animal leave fur on tree trunks/limbs from repeated scratching and rubbing?
- Does the animal markup trees and remove bark with antlers or tusks from repeated rubbing?
- Does the animal travel in herds, small family units, or are they solitary?
- Does the animal tend to live in specific areas like grasslands, forests, or near running water?
- Does the animal migrate?
- Does the animal have a distinctive call (sound) and are they attracted to certain sounds (distress or mating) or smells?

Once you are able to discern those types of answers, you'll need to know if the animal is suitable for trapping or hunting. Most of your small game is suitable for trapping but you'll need to know which kind of trap or snare works best on which animals.

The most widely used devices today are:

- Foothold
- Conibear
- Snares
- Live Trap (cages)

The good news about modern traps and snares is that they are relatively inexpensive so you could conceivably become quite well stocked in fairly short order. Additionally, doing a basic internet search for the term 'primitive traps' will yield a wealth of additional information that you could utilize as well.

Foraging

Foraging is an art form, plain and simple. Successfully foraging for specific greens, plants, trees, flowers, roots, berries, etc. means that you need to know very specific information regarding each. For example, you'll need to know where it grows, what it looks like, any look-a-likes that are poisonous, and how to prepare and store what is collected.

It is also important to know which collected material is suitable for eating and which are best suited for their medicinal properties.

Here are some resources that you might want to consider reviewing and/or purchasing to aid you in this endeavor:

- 21 Native Wild Edible Plants by Mors Kochanski
- A Field Guide to Medicinal Plants and Herbs: Of Eastern/Central North America (Peterson Field Guides) by Steven Foster and James A. Duke
- Edible Wild Plants: A North American Field Guide to Over 200 Natural Foods by Thomas Elias and Peter Dykeman
- Medicinal Plants and Herbs (Eastern Central Region) by Peterson Field Guides (find the book related to your region)
- The Forager's Harvest - A Guide to Identifying, Harvesting, and Preparing Edible Wild Plants by Samuel Thayer
- Regional Foraging Series

Silent Hunt

When it comes to trying to locate and procure wild game (large and small), you might want to consider a weapon that makes very little noise. As an example, a lone weapon report can be heard for miles. Why would you willingly announce your presence by using a firearm in a major disruption when not engaged with another person using a weapon? Not only will that fired weapon tell any wildlife that you may not have seen that you are there, but it will also alert any human within earshot that someone potentially has something worth taking by force.

In order to solve this issue, consider only using firearms for defensive purposes and contemplate the inclusion of some of the following:

- Air rifle
- Compound bow
- Crossbow
- Crossbow pistol
- Recurve bow
- Slingshot
- Weighted nets

I would avoid any air rifle that requires a compressed CO_2 cartridge as it is a consumable. Focus instead on an air rifle that you pump yourself. Ammunition for a slingshot can be found on the ground in the form or small rocks. Extra bowstring can be stockpiled for cheap but compound bows and crossbows will require a bow press (either a field press or a bow stand) in order to restring. The weighted nets could be used for fishing and for capturing birds swimming or nesting together.

Beekeeping

I would highly recommend that you begin learning everything you can about the skillset of beekeeping. If you want a successful vegetable garden, orchard, and medicinal garden you are going to need pollinators. Having a couple beehives will definitely help to ensure a successful harvest. The general rule of thumb is 1-2 hives per acre. Personally, I think it would be preferable to stack the deck in your favor and have your own source of pollinators as opposed to relying solely on the whims of Mother Nature, which can be fickle at times.

Mother Nature isn't the only fickle thing about incorporating beehives though. Most city and town ordinances prohibit the housing of bee colonies on your property within city limits. Therefore, this approach is really best suited for those that are not subject to zoning and HOA rules.

Doing a basic web search for the term 'beekeeper training' will yield a wide variety of options available to you in your area for acquiring this skillset. Some classes are online while others can be attended in person at college extensions or beekeeper clubs.

Additionally, you can contact established beekeepers in your area, rent hive boxes, and share in the spoils of the collected honey. Having access to a decent supply of honey is extremely beneficial as the by-product of all that pollination is a natural sweetener as well as a highly valuable medicinal ingredient.

Livestock

Most city ordinances and HOA agreements will prohibit the keeping of livestock on your property in an urban or suburban setting. Therefore, this suggestion is only for those with appreciable land reserves and where restrictive zoning covenants do not apply. Don't let the term 'livestock' fool you though. It doesn't only apply to large animals like cows and pigs.

The key to incorporating livestock into your major disruption plans is to choose animals that serve multiple purposes and that can survive in your location. Meaning, some animals don't like prolonged periods of excessive heat (summer), cold (winter), dry, or wet climates. You'll need to either address as many issues as possible via shelters, plentiful water, and bedding materials, or choose a different species of that animal more indigenous or compatible to that area. Don't just plan to use a heater or heat lamps for cold weather warmth in good times because neither may be available to you in a bad time (major disruption). The adaptability of the animal is a major contributing factor to its inclusion in your plans.

Here's a list of possible livestock options that require very little space (as opposed to cattle, horses, pigs, etc.), feed, and water that can be raised in a sustainable manner to compliment the wild protein resources (hunting, trapping, fishing, etc.) available to you:

- Chicken (meat, eggs, fat)
- Duck (meat, eggs)
- Fish (meat, oil)
- Goat (meat, milk, fat)
- Goose (meat, eggs, fat)
- Grouse (meat)
- Pheasant (meat, eggs)
- Quail (meat, eggs, fat)
- Rabbit (meat)
- Sheep (meat, wool)
- Turkey (meat, eggs, fat)

Do some research on each animal and the various species within that classification to learn more about raising each and their specific needs when it comes to space, feed, water, breeding, production, etc. Beyond that you need to learn how to process and breakdown each animal and have the necessary tools and implements for maintenance. I would seriously consider a feather-plucking machine if you opt for any of the birds noted above. You'll need to convert any electric models to a hand-crank model to utilize this tool in a major disruption. They do make plucking attachments for your drill so this may be an option if you can keep a battery charged.

If you have the space, having a milk cow or two would be extremely beneficial as well for meat, milk, fat, and draft (plow). As would some horses for transportation and draft purposes too. Before exchanging money on these larger purchases though, ask for a demonstration to observe temperament and be prepared to bring an independent third-party veterinarian with you to verify the health and condition of the animal(s) being considered.

You can find all manner of information on these animals by going to Amazon and looking for books on "Raising [insert animal name here]" and 'Animal Husbandry.'

Fire

When it comes to the topic of 'fire' in a major disruption, please review the *Fire* sections in Chapter 3 and Chapter 4 as all of that previously included information is wholly applicable in a major disruption. However, there is one thing I'd like to mention which could be handled in the Basics concept of either Fire or Food and that is a good wood burning stove.

If you are planning to prepare for a major disruption then you need to own up to the reality that any liquid fuel you may have stored is going to be exhausted eventually. Your city's natural gas feed won't likely stay pressurized either.

You will need to learn two things in terms of fire for this duration.

1. Learn how to cook with wood.
2. Learn how to make charcoal.

Wood Burning Stoves

Cooking with wood and an open flame isn't very dissimilar to cooking on a charcoal grill before the disruption. You still have to watch the coals, move the wood and coals around to cook with direct or indirect heat. Those concepts and principles haven't changed. The real test comes when you try to cook with a wood burning stove.

There are a number of quality manufacturers out there so do your research and find the model and manufacturer that checks off the most boxes in terms of number of grates (or plates), firebox size, oven, etc. Be careful in your research though. A wood burning stove serves two purposes. The first is obviously to cook with as a potential replacement for your gas or electric stove. The other is as a heat source.

Some wood burning stoves are geared more toward functioning as a heat source first and a cooking surface second. Sometimes they are referred to as camp stoves, which only adds to the confusion of the single and dual burner gas stoves used when camping. These wood burning stoves tend to be smaller, portable, and generally only have the capability to handle one pan or two (or coffee pot) at a time. From experience, I can tell you that the smaller wood burning stoves in this example are best suited for smaller square foot spaces like a tent or small shed/cabin.

Wood stoves that are smaller and portable can be found for a few hundred dollars at your bigger box stores like Lowes and Home Depot as well as places like Tractor Supply, Cabela's, Field & Stream, and Bass Pro Shop. You can order one online and have it delivered easily or, if you prefer, you can go to your small town hardware store and have them order one for you. Remember to support local merchants whenever possible.

Regardless of whether or not you plan to shelter in place or relocate to a different well-stocked, secluded location, you are likely going to want a larger wood cook stove though. The reason for this is simple, quantity. A dedicated and stationary wood cook stove will allow you to cook multiple items at once while also baking. This is what you are going to need if you're cooking for a single nuclear family of four or a larger group. What you are looking for depends on your situation, size of the space, and number of people.

A good stationary wood burning cook stove brand new can be expensive as prices range from $1,000.00 to $7,000.00 depending on the manufacturer and your needs. Here are some links that will help you gain some more information on wood burning cook stoves:

- https://www.discountstoves.net/wood-cook-stoves-s/37.htm
- https://www.remodelista.com/posts/5-favorites-wood-cook-stoves/
- https://www.woodcookstove.com/wood-burning-cook-stoves.html
- https://www.5dog.farm/my-kingdom-for-a-cookstove/
- https://joybileefarm.com/perfect-wood-cook-stove/

Charcoal

Outside of learning how to cook again, you'll also want to learn how to make charcoal. Making charcoal is a straightforward process. Burn the wood to the point that you remove any organic material then restrict its access to oxygen. What you're left with is pure carbon. The charcoal can be used in a furnace by a blacksmith and in your woodstove for cooking.

Here are some links that will help you gain some more information on making charcoal:

- https://www.smokedbbqsource.com/how-to-make-charcoal/
- https://www.popularmechanics.com/home/outdoor-projects/a28848441/how-to-make-charcoal/
- https://urbansurvivalsite.com/9-easy-steps-make-charcoal/
- https://www.resilience.org/stories/2018-08-14/making-charcoal/
- https://survivial-training.wonderhowto.com/how-to/make-your-own-charcoal-0148846/

Woodlot

The concept of a woodlot is only going to pertain to those in a rural area with timbered acreage on their land, or nearby after a disruption (national/state forest). For those not in the know, a woodlot is a parcel of woodland or forest capable of producing:

- Wood fuel
- Sap for syrups
- Medicinal ingredients (bark, roots, flowers)
- Sawlogs (if you have a sawmill, portable or other)
  - Lumber for bartering
  - Lumber for buildings
  - Lumber for furniture

A woodlot can also be a long narrow buffer between farms or some form of development, like a hedgerow of sorts. Prior to planning for a major disruption, this forested acreage probably went untouched except for the occasional tapping or felling of a tree for some free maple syrup or firewood. However, in order to plan for a major disruption, you need to be actively working your woodlot.

This means felling dead, diseased, and scrub trees as well as removing native and non-native underbrush not needed for medicinal remedies. All of this material is kindling to a forest fire. Leave some plant material to help prevent erosion though. After that, you'll want to observe the spacing (possibly remove (thin) some trees to promote better, stronger, straighter growth), identify the trees (determine what species are available to you), and scout the area (wildlife habitat).

Here are some links that will help you gain some more information on woodlots:

- https://www.youtube.com/watch?v=Dd1PwIoH7dg (video)
- https://practicalselfreliance.com/medicinal-trees/
- https://www.agriculture.com/family/living-the-country-life/managing-your-woodlot
- https://www.motherearthnews.com/homesteading-and-livestock/woodlot-management-zmaz95fmztak

Smokehouse

While a smokehouse could be addressed in the *Food* section, its construction and use in a major disruption also falls into the *Fire* category. The reason I've included here in the *Fire* section is that the process for smoking meat, birds, and fish for long-term storage requires yet another approach to the use of fire. A smokehouse doesn't cook the items per se, but rather, uses the smoke from a slow burning hardwood fire to cure and dry the meat, bird, and fish.

The fire used in this process is located outside of the structure in a firebox. The smokehouse structure itself is windowless and has a simple vent to control the smoke flow and temperature. The firebox is connected to the structure via piping which allows the smoke and some heat to be pulled into the structure from the bottom of the structure. The smoke and heat will waft upwards toward, and through, the hanging meat, bird, and/or fish before being vented out. Curing and drying meat and fish falls into that category known as low and slow cooking

Here are some resources to learn more about smokehouses:

- A Guide to Canning, Freezing, Curing & Smoking Meat, Fish & Game by Wilbur F. Eastman
- Meat Smoking and Smokehouse Design by Adam & Stanley Marianski
- https://www.youtube.com/watch?v=UjsqfSbK1ro (Video #1 - Foundation)
- https://www.youtube.com/watch?v=zaVcTYfWBGQ (Video #2 - Flue and Block)
- https://www.youtube.com/watch?v=ySi1HEeUN6Q (Video #3 - Fire Box)
- https://www.youtube.com/watch?v=2rNRxTekOV8 (Video #4 - Roof and Frame)
- https://www.youtube.com/watch?v=vZpD3FKwn4s (Video #5 - Final Touches)

***

Now that we've taken an even deeper dive in to three of the concepts comprising the Basics, let's dig in to some of the topics we've already discussed in location & security as well as some of the other topics I've mentioned previously. These topics include medicinal herbs, portability, and bartering.

***

Location & Security

When it comes to location and security, there are a number of things that will factor into your decision making process. The first of which I mentioned previously and that is distance from major population centers. Beyond that though, among other things, you're going to want to consider:

- Climate
- Communication
- Defensibility
- Elevation
- Soil Composition
- Resource Availability

Defensibility is on this list because if there is a major disruption and resources are limited and/or the rule of law is spotty at best, people *will* get desperate and people *will* try and potentially take what you have, sometimes by force.

A great number of factors should be considered when determining your ultimate location and the level of security you are willing to employ. The cost of the land, property taxes, tax exemptions, state laws governing homesteading, water resources, growing conditions, etc. all factor into choosing a location. The topics I've chosen to include are not all-inclusive. *Location and Security* is very subjective but what is included here is merely designed to get your gears turning, so to speak, in terms of topics, considerations, and obstacles that need to be considered.

Let's take a brief look at each of these topics.

Climate

If you are planning to settle somewhere else permanently, or if you are planning a backup location should you need to relocate in a hurry, you need to consider the destination climate. If it is dry and arid with little rainfall, you need to be planning accordingly. This means livestock, water harvesting, gardening, and clothing, all of it. Conversely, if the climate is moist, you need to plan accordingly for each of the items I just mentioned, but you also need to think about water abatement.

You must consider the climate or you'll never survive a major disruption intact. You need to do some research on the area you are considering *before* you purchase anything. Don't just wing it and hope for the best. That means, you need the following to make the best decision possible:

- Average precipitation (rain and snow)
- Average temperature (high and low)
- Coldest/hottest month(s)
- Drainage (soil composition)
- Risks (flash floods, forest fires, mud slides, earthquakes, tornados, hurricanes)
- Watershed (movement of water)

Communication

Having a means to communicate across your property, with family/group members, with neighbors and a nearby small town, as well as the ability to hear news from independent HAM operators at distance is paramount in a major disruption situation.

Therefore, I highly recommend that you look into low wattage CB's for basic two-way communication for shorter distances, a stationary HAM radio for listening and/or conversation (requires a license when rule of law exists) over longer distances, rechargeable hand-held walkies with ear wigs. Baofeng makes a hand-held HAM walkie ($90 on Amazon) that is excellent for moderate distances and it could be utilized for longer distances if there was enough power behind it and the atmospherics were optimal.

Beyond that, if you have fixed, dug-in positions like an observation post/listening post (OP/LP), think about purchasing old military gear and comm wire to run between the main structure and the LP/OP as well as potentially any out buildings. This option is the only secure form of communication available short of a hand written message utilizing a code or a programmable oscillator for your comm gear. Just about all aerial/wireless options are subject to eavesdropping and interception. So be careful. Loose lips sinks ships isn't just a catchy phrase.

Prior to an event of any duration, I would highly recommend training for HAM radio operation. There is a great deal of information that you need to know for this skillset like specific frequencies, how radio transmissions work, how the atmosphere can help/hinder transmissions, etc. The good news is that there are HAM operators everywhere and most are willing to help and train new operators. Beyond that, you can use the following resources to learn more about communication, where to find training, etc.:

- http://www.arrl.org/courses-training
- http://www.arrl.org/find-an-amateur-radio-license-class
- http://www.arrl.org/ham-radio-licenses

There are other sites available where you pay for training and they are relatively inexpensive, $25.00-$50.00 per course.

Defensibility

Look at the terrain for the location you're considering and then think like a gang leader about how you would gain access and steal everything you own. From there, start planning and strategizing a means to handle each potential option or scenario you discovered, or choose a different more defensible property for purchase.

At a minimum, you'll need to consider where:

- Buildings, equipment, and livestock are positioned
- Ingress, egress, and choke points are located
- Natural draws and terrain elevation changes
- Proximity to roads, towns, neighbors, etc.
- Sightline obstructions

Once you've considered all of that, think about the best place to see and hear the furthest using the concealment of an observation post/listening post (OP/LP). Incorporating an LP/OP will allow the person manning the structure to provide advanced warning, preferably via secure communication, of any potential issues.

The topic of *Defensibility* also entails the means to defend oneself and ones property from intrusion. A good long range weapon like a hunting rifle can diffuse situations from distance while closer quarter weapons like pistols and semi-automatic rifles are helpful should someone, or a group of someone's, make it inside your perimeter. A riot shotgun works well inside buildings as any of the missed shot is not likely to travel beyond a wall it impacts. A bullet on the other hand will, travel through not only the target and/or wall but will, likely exit the home entirely. Bladed edge weapons are good for this use as well.

I highly recommend the inclusion of firearms, knife fighting and maintenance, and general self-defense training into your planning for a major disruption. The incorporation of various traps and warning indicators (ex. trip flares, tannerite, spider holes, etc.) would be of use too.

Elevation

Choosing a location with elevation gradients is necessary if you plan to incorporate well-fed cisterns, gravity fed water in the home, and man-made water features like ponds and overflow streams on your property. Elevation becomes an issue if you need to transport the water from a natural source on your property either through physical or mechanical means. So choose your property/location wisely and have a proven plan to address any elevation differences. Altitude is another matter entirely.

Elevation also needs to be considered when you are contemplating the defensibility of the property. Try approaching the main structure from various vantage points to gauge the difficulty of the task and them implement various remedies to make that approach that much more difficult for an intruder.

Soil Composition

The composition of the soil goes the very heart of the survivability of the people residing on the property. It also plays a crucial role in the selection of livestock. Too much underlying rock and clay and the soil will drain very slowly and you'll be left with boggy marsh-like areas. Too much sand and the soil will drain too quickly and take all of the vital nutrients with the retreating water.

Review the *Homemade Soil Test* section of Chapter 4 and be prepared to do a few soil tests on the fly when inspecting potential property.

Additionally, be prepared to have a geologic survey done on the property. Geologic maps show the distribution, composition, and age of the rocks and sediments. These maps will aid you in making a better more informed decision.

State, county, and town specific geologic area maps can be found by doing a search on the USGS website [Full URL: https://ngmdb.usgs.gov/ngm-bin/ngm_compsearch.pl]. Unfortunately, property specific data will require a dedicated geologic survey.

Resource Availability

Resource availability goes back to what I wrote in the *Available Food Sources* section of this chapter. You need to survey your potential purchase for animal sign, different types of frequented food plots for any wildlife in the area, fresh water reserves, etc. If the resources just aren't there but have been in the past, then consider ways to attract them back to the area with water sources, food plots, plantings, etc. or consider a different property with more resources.

Training

To piggy-back on the *Defensibility* topic, you will want to consider increasing your skill set with firearms through dedicated training from professionals. The safe handling of a weapon is paramount when it comes to owning any firearm.

When it comes to pistols, for example, each state is different. Some have open-carry laws while most, if not all, require a specific number of hours of training (classroom and range) before the issuance of a concealed carry license. Here's a URL for a comprehensive guide to various state gun laws: https://www.nraila.org/gun-laws/

Unfortunately, some states have also started implementing a third uncodified criterion, which is 'need.' As in, you must prove why you need a concealed carry license and/or weapon to the issuing agency, usually a county sheriff department. This is a European approach to personal protection and many oppose this as an infringement of rights. Regardless, on top of the 'need' based assessment, which may or may not be occurring, the cost of a license is steadily climbing in some states. There are many theories as to why as some say it's merely supply and demand, while others view it as an effort to curtail gun violence by limiting access. Others still have taken to believing that states are trying to infringe on the Second Amendment by proxy via cost (taxation). Some states though, simply don't process the application in a timely manner preferring instead to let applicants languish in limbo. Here's an article about that. [Full URL:

https://www.nraila.org/articles/20210104/new-york-city-demonstrates-the-danger-to-freedom-and-safety-of-firearm-licensing-laws]

If you find yourself in a state that doesn't put a premium on personal freedoms and you value your ability to protect yourself, your family, and your property, I would seriously consider relocating to a state that does.

Outside of a conceal carry license, when it comes to training you'll want to consider several other forms of training like marksmanship, weapon maintenance, and scenario driven drills. Doing a basic web search for terms similar to 'marksmanship training near me' or 'firearms training near me' will yield considerable results. Additionally, your local gun store likely has classroom training sessions available for weapon maintenance training. This is extremely beneficial for first time buyers. If you were raised on shotgun/rifle hunting but don't use pistols all that much, or vice versa, this form of training will help you too. I would not rely of YouTube how-to videos for this level of instruction.

Here are some resources that might be of use to you as you seek out various forms of firearms training:

- Front Sight: https://www.frontsight.com/Courses.asp
- Project Appleseed: https://appleseedinfo.org/
- Valor Ridge: https://www.valorridge.com/pages/classes

Beyond the training, if you're serious about defensibility, you might want to consider applying for a Federal Firearms License (FFL). Having an FFL allows you to be a destination source for firearms being bought and shipped across state lines, potentially run 4473 Firearm Transaction Record background checks, and may allow you to purchase firearms at a reduced cost directly from the manufacturer. If you are part of a group, being able to buy multiple weapons at the same time for a reduced cost has benefits beyond cost too. This will insure that everyone has a group standard weapon where parts, magazines, and ammunition are all compatible as well.

When it comes to determining a standard weapon if you're in a group environment, you need to consider age, gender, ammunition prices, as well availability of parts and ammo and any potential reloading costs. I would avoid rare or odd calibers weapons for any group standard weapons.

Topographic Maps

National Geographic has a website where you can zoom in on a particular location and generate your own topographic maps. [Full URL: https://www.natgeomaps.com/trail-maps/pdf-quads]. This is an excellent resource for getting the lay of the land very quickly before you arrive on the property to inspect it. Generating and reviewing these detailed area maps will aid you in answering some questions regarding 'defensibility' and 'elevation' and can give you a head start in answering questions regarding 'soil composition' and 'resource availability' too.

Reloading

Reloading ammunition is a cost effective time-honored tradition for many who hunt and target shoot a lot. Unfortunately, the startup costs can be a bit much (reloading press, dies) but once you're up and running it is a very therapeutic way to spend some down time.

The first thing you'll need to know is what do you want to reload. Do you want to reload shotgun shells (ex. 10, 12, 20, 410 gauge), rifle (ex. .223, 30-06, .308), or pistol (ex. 9mm, 45ACP, .357) cartridges?

Answering the above question regarding what you'd like to reload is vitally important as different presses and dies are utilized for different types of ammunition. As a result, I highly recommend that you do as much research as possible on the type(s) of ammo you want to reload before buying anything associated with reloading. After that, go find someone that you know that reloads and ask them to train you or is willing to let you practice under their guidance then do a web search for the term 'reloading training near me' for further instruction.

Here are some resources for you to learn more about the reloading process and reloading presses:

- https://www.pewpewtactical.com/best-reloading-presses-beginners/
- https://leeprecision.com/reloading-presses/
- https://www.rcbs.com/
- https://www.hornady.com/reloading/presses/

Medical

When planning for a major disruption, having someone, either in your family or in your group, that is trained in medicine would be beyond beneficial. Think about all of things that could befall you or a family member on a daily basis pre-disruption and then amplify it. That's what life in a major disruption could potentially be like.

Now, short of training certificates and degrees earned, medical supplies must be kept on hand in preparation for any disturbance duration. Most everything you'll generally encounter can be handled with a robust first aid kit. These are available online just about everywhere and in every store carrying supplies. There are also specific 'add-on' kits available for burns, surgical, and dentistry. Beyond the robust first aid kits, you might want to consider adding the following, which may or may not have been in the first aid kit or in the kit add-on:

- Acetaminophen/Ibuprofen (exp. dates require stock rotation)
- Alcohol Swabs
- Bandages/Wraps (Ace, Israeli, assorted width/length)
- Band-Aids (boxes upon boxes)
- Betadine (iodine solution)
- Blood Typing Family Cross Reference Sheet
- Braces (knee, ankle, wrist)
- Butterfly Bandages
- Chest Seal
- Creams (antibiotic, burn, itch, yeast)
- Gauze
- Gloves (assorted sizes with/without latex)
- Kit Add-On (burn, dentistry, surgical)
- Masks
- Peroxide
- Petroleum Jelly
- Quikclot (Celox or similar)
- Tape (rolls upon rolls)
- Thermometer
- Tools (clamps, scalpels, forceps, tweezers, dental, etc.)
- Tourniquet
- Tubing
- Suture Material (needle and thread (ex. 3.0 silk))

Lastly, as I've stated previously, this is not an exhaustive list by any means. As your skills increase in this area or specialty, so will you'll knowledge base as it pertains to the supplies you personally want available to you in an emergency. Use the list as a guide and build upon it.

Training

It is understood that medical training is necessary for this topic. Short of becoming a nurse or doctor, you can get a number of lower level certifications and receive some very beneficial hands-on training using the following resources:

- https://www.redcross.org/take-a-class
- https://www.procpr.org/training
- https://emergencycare.hsi.com/cpr-and-first-aid-courses

Medicinal Herbs

Every single item, short of the denoted tools and assorted wraps, mentioned in the *Medical* section is a consumable. Therefore, eventually, they will be exhausted as a resource. This means you're going to have to figure other, possibly more natural, ways to handle various ailments. This is where the medicinal herb garden comes into play.

Medicinal herbs were used for centuries in every civilization since the dawn of time. It's only in the last seventy-five years or so that we've had the Big Pharma industry. The difference between the two is usually the amount of time that transpires between the initial treatment and a full recovery.

I would highly recommend keeping hard copy paperback books on your shelf in the event of a major disruption. Avoid the inclination to purchase electronic versions (Kindle) of these resources. That being said, here are some resources you might want to aid to your bookshelf:

- Home Remedies, Poultices, Salves & Tinctures by David J Kershner
- Prepper's Natural Medicine: Life-Saving Herbs, Essential Oils and Natural Remedies for When There is No Doctor by Cat Ellis
- Where There Is No Doctor: A Village Health Care Handbook by David Werner and Carol Thuman
- Where There Is No Dentist by Murray Dickson

Here's some information of five of the most widely used medicinal herbs:

Echinacea

Used as an antibiotic to treat scarlet fever, syphilis, malaria, blood poisoning, and diphtheria, but it can also enhance the activity of the immune system, relieve pain, and reduce inflammation. It has hormonal, antiviral, and antioxidant effects too. Professional herbalists recommend Echinacea to treat UTI's, vaginal and ear infections, athlete's foot, sinusitis, hay fever, as well as slow-healing wounds.

Pleurisy Root

Native Americans claim that it is good for lifting and running strength, but can also be used to handle poopy problems like diarrhea and dysentery. It also serves as an expectorant. This makes it a valuable medicinal herb for chest complaints and in the treatment of many lung diseases.

Lemon Balm

Used extensively in the treatment of fever, colic, mumps, cold sores, and other viruses. The anti-viral agent has researchers looking into its usefulness for Chronic Fatigue Syndrome and Shingles. One of lemon balm's key medicinal attributes is as a tranquilizer, or mild sedative, and it calms a nervous stomach, colic, or heart spasms. Some people think that the leaves aid in lowering blood pressure. It is very gentle, but effective, which is why herbalists use it extensively for children and babies. Moreover, it has anti-histamine properties so it's useful to treat eczema and headaches, as well as insect bites and wounds. More recently though, scientists have discovered that lemon balm affects the limbic system of the brain so it was added to the ADHD formula.

Nettle

Known as the 'woman's herb' for relieving menstrual cramps and a wide variety of other ailments by many ancient civilizations. Additional uses include the treatment of asthma, as well as allergy and cold relief (loosens congestion). It is generally regarded as a diuretic and promotes kidney health and function. The stalks of the plant were once used to make cloth while the leaves, while rich in nutrients as they contain a wide variety of vitamins and minerals, were often used as a substitute green for cooking. If you can figure out a way to juice it, nettle is natural bug repellant.

Hyssop & Catnip

Both are used for cold and flu, but hyssop can also address sore throats, bruises, and burns while catnip addresses headaches and fever. Using a modern day analogy, herbalist may have alternated the use of both for a patient much like we alternate between Tylenol and ibuprofen.

Portability

Planning for a major disruption means different things to different people. For example, some plan to stay where they are (shelter in place) and defend what's theirs come hell or high water. Others will plan to move to a more secure and secluded location (bugging out or Getting out of Dodge (G.O.O.D)). Unfortunately, if the rule of law has collapsed during the course of a major disruption you're best laid plans may need rapid adjustment. Planning for this possibility makes good (and common) sense.

If your plan is to bugout to a safe place, or you're being forced to evacuate, reliable vehicle(s) and fuel is/are a must. Keeping your vehicles in good working order is paramount. Preferably, I'd recommend you invest in a solidly built 4WD model where parts are interchangeable and can be easily sourced, scavenged, or cannibalized depending on the situation.

However, what happens if the car breaks down or you run out of gas? What happens if you're forced to carry on to your destination the rest of the way on foot? Things are going to deteriorate in a hurry if you haven't thought to:

- Cache and pre-positioned some of your supplies
- Consider the weight of what you're planning to carry

To put it another way, the weight, quantity, and your ability to move it with ease is going to be final determining factor for what goes and what stays if you're on foot. Period.

Let's look at some common things you might have with you... you know, things like:

- Ammo (assorted popular calibers)
  - 22 LR (36 gr) – 0.75 lbs per 100 rds
  - 9 mm (115 gr) – 2.63 lbs per 100 rds.
  - 223/5.56x45 (63 gr) – 2.69 lbs per 100 rds
  - 40 S&W – 3.56 lbs per 100 rds.
  - 45 ACP (230 gr) – 4.69 lbs. per 100 rds.
- Camping Stoves
  - Single/Dual burner
  - Fuel canisters
- Food
  - Assorted canned goods
  - Home canned (glass)
  - Home canned (5 gal tubs)
  - Freeze Dried
- Fuel (various)
  - Regular - 6 lbs per gallon
  - Diesel – 7.6 lbs per gallon
  - Propane – 4.25 lbs per gallon
  - Kerosene – 6.82 lbs per gallon
- Propane Tanks – 37 lbs per tank
- Keepsakes
- Sleeping bags
- Tents
- Water - 8.34 lbs per gallon
- Weapons

To help you understand the need for caching, prioritized packing, and the weight of it all, Graywolf Survival posted an article detailing a 25 lb. pack loaded with a wide assortment of items that can help you ultimately make it safely to your destination, assuming you pre-positioned resources at your final destination. [Full URL: http://graywolfsurvival.com/66545/how-to-build-ultimate-25-pound-bug-bag/]

Carrying something with that much useful stuff, and only weighs as much as a two year old, could save your life.

Barter - Currency Options

Most people will agree that in the event of a major disruption coupled with a potential societal collapse, government backed paper currency will become useless. If that is in fact the case, then what? What will you do for currency?

First, you have to look at how you are actually defining the word 'currency.' To different people with different backgrounds in different regions, 'currency' be defined as a:

- <u>Tangible Commodity</u>: Items that contain some sort of intrinsic monetary value. Example: bars, coins, and nuggets made from precious metals like gold, silver, platinum, or possibly even gems and stones.
- <u>Equivalent Value</u>: Items that can be bartered or swapped in a like for like scenario. Example: food, water, weapons/ammo, blade weapons, clothing, seeds, canning supplies, thread, etc.
- <u>Tradeable Skill</u>: Item that is exchanged for services. Example: room/board/food for security or field work, paying for a service like shoeing horses, general blacksmithing, medical or veterinary expertise, prostitution, carpentry, plumbing, electrical, etc.

It is my belief that *ALL* of these can be valued as 'currency' during a major disruption. It really depends on what the individuals involved in the bartered arrangement are willing to trade.

Let's take a closer look at each of these currency types individually to see where and how one, two, or all of them could be utilized by you and your family.

Tangible Commodity

If you're considering the inclusion of gold, silver, etc then you will need to plan years ahead and budget accordingly as none of these options are on the inexpensive side of the scale. Before you go to the bank and start procuring roll after roll of quarters, dimes, and nickels here's what the US Mint has to say regarding the specifics for each modern coin they manufacture:

Modern Coinage Weight & Composition Table

Denomination	Composition	Weight
Cent	Copper Plated Zinc (Zn) 2.5% Copper (Cu) Balance Zinc	2.500 g
Nickel	Cupro-Nickel 25% Nickel (Ni) Balance Copper	5.000 g
Dime	Cupro-Nickel 8.33% Nickel (Ni) Balance Copper	2.268 g
Quarter	Cupro-Nickel 8.33% Nickel (Ni) Balance Copper	5.670 g
Half Dollar	Cupro-Nickel 8.33 Nickel (Ni) Balance Copper	11.340 g
Presidential $1	Manganese-Brass 88.5% Copper (Cu) 6% Zinc (Zn) 3.5% Manganese (Mn) 2% Nickel (Ni)	8.1 g

As you can see from the table, today's modern coinage contains exactly **zero** silver. If any of these coins did, you'd see the periodic table symbol 'Ag' in the Composition column. Today's coins are essentially knock-offs. They look, feel, and weigh the same but in terms of using a modern coin for its precious metal content, there isn't any. In fact, the US Mint hasn't used silver in its composition since the mid-1960's when they went from 90% silver and 10% copper to an all copper-nickel alloy.

Here's a more thorough run down on when each denomination was changed from silver to the copper-alloy:

- Nickels
  - Jefferson Wartime (1942 (partial)-1945) – 35% silver
- Dimes
  - Liberty Head "Barber" (1892-1916) – 90% silver
  - Winged Liberty Head "Mercury" (1916-1945) – 90% silver
  - Roosevelt (1946-1964) – 90% silver
- Quarters
  - Liberty Head "Barber" (1892-1916) – 90% silver
  - Standing Liberty (1916-1930) – 90% silver
  - Washington (1932, 1934-1964) – 90% silver
- Half Dollars
  - Liberty Head "Barber" (1892-1915) – 90% silver
  - Walking Liberty (1916-1947) – 90% silver
  - Franklin (1948-1963) – 90% silver
  - Kennedy (1964) – 90% silver
  - Kennedy (1965-1970) – 40% silver
- Dollars
  - Morgan (1878-1904, 1921) – 90% silver
  - Peace (1921-1928, 1934-1935) – 90% silver

In order to locate common coins (nickels, dimes, quarters) containing silver (meaning pre-1965), you could visit flea markets, swaps, private sellers, garage sales, and hope for the best or you could utilize websites and possibly banks. However, if you're going to go the website route, you need to make sure they are reputable dealers. A simple online search revealed these options:

- Apmex
- JM Bullion
- Provident Metals

Personally, I use JM Bullion for no other reason than they had the most information and the largest selection.

From the sites I provided, you can view, compare, and purchase gold and silver coins and bars as well as platinum, copper, rounds, and bags of 90% and 40% junk coins. The bags of 'junk' coins are coins the US Mint used to create before the 1960's. Also, don't be so quick to dismiss non-gold and silver metals.

Do yourself a favor and don't limit yourself to coins exclusively. Many items currently in use contain silver. Here's a link to an article that explains where you can find these items and why you shouldn't be selling grandma's silver [Full URL: https://www.star-telegram.com/news/business/article3840991.html]

In February of 2016, I wrote an article about this topic and I included the current price (02/16/2016) per ounce for several types of precious metals. Below is a comparison for where we were just four years ago and where the prices are now (12/30/2020). I should note that copper is priced by the pound and many scrap metals dealers' payout by the pound as well. It is for this reason alone that thieves steal so much of it.

Precious Metal Four Year Comparison

Metal Type	2016 Cost Per Oz.	2020 Cost Per Oz.	Price Per Oz. Increase
Gold	$1206.20	$1894.00	$687.80
Silver	$15.33	$26.50	$11.17
Copper	$2.05 (per lb.)	$2.85 (per lb.)	$0.80
Platinum	$932.10	$1077.10	$145.00
Palladium	$508.90	$2395.77	$1886.87

Silver is by far the most economical, but don't discount copper. It is a very good material if you're planning on making things for trade or have the ability to create casts or forms for bullets.

The only thing you need to know now is the equivalent. By that I mean, when you go looking at bars of silver, gold, platinum, palladium, or copper (as opposed to coins for example), you need to know what the actual weight of a nickel, dime, or quarter are so you can estimate/compare size and value. This information was contained in the third column of the *Modern Coinage Weight & Composition Table*.

Personally, I like silver, but to be specific I like the 5g and 10g bars. I find that the bags of junk silver are a good purchase but the price point means you likely aren't buying many of these bags. A gold bar here or there doesn't hurt either, but they're currently asking $80.00 per 1g bar. I can get a 5g bar of silver (same weight as a nickel) for $7.00.

If we move cost analysis to the side and focus on science, silver (and copper for that matter) has a lower melting point and can be fashioned into far more than gold. However, gold is generally understood as the most valuable of the precious metals as platinum and palladium are not in wide circulation.

Equivalent Value

When most people think of the word 'barter,' they think 'trade,' or 'like-for-like.' Below is a list of items that you might want to consider having for bartering purposes should the need arise:

- Alcohol (airplane bottle size)
- Aluminum Foil
- Ammunition (assorted calibers/gauges)
- Beeswax (several pounds)
- Cable Rolls (assorted thickness, cable clamps)
- Candle making Supplies (wax and wicking)
- Canning Supplies (rims, lids)
- Condoms
- Duct Tape (muted colors)
- Engine/Fuel oil (2 and 4 cycle)
- Gas stabilizer/Diesel antibacterial additive
- Honey (assorted sized bottles)
- Feminine Hygiene (Diva Cup, pads, tampons)
- Fishing Gear (line, weights, nets, lures)
- Fuel (gas, diesel, kerosene, spare 1-gallon cans)
- Laundry Detergent
- Lubricant (firearms, vehicles, machinery)
- Matches (all-weather, strike anywhere)
- Medical Supplies (bandages, compresses, wraps, tubing, tools)
- Pans (pie, bread, baking)
- Reloading Supplies (primers, wad, powder, shot, bullets, brass)
- Rolls of Plastic
- Rope/String/Paracord (muted colors)
- Salt (blocks, bags, canisters, packets)
- Sewing supplies (thread, needle, patch material, belts)
- Spices (cooking, curing)
- Tobacco
- Wire Rolls (plain, barbed, chicken, rabbit, chain link)

Please bear in mind that this is not an exhaustive list. What you should do is review this list and think about what would be of value to you or within your community in the event of a major disruption. What you should *not* do is advertise you have any of it on hand.

Tradeable Skill or Service

Suppose you don't have any coin, gold, or silver and you've left someplace in such a hurry that you literally only have the clothes on your back and maybe a can of beans. What now? Well, now you need to make sure you have a skill or can provide a service in exchange for food or shelter or both. The following list isn't all-inclusive by any means, but it will give you a fair idea with regard to what skills might be needed to outlast a major disruption. Oh, and take this list with a grain of salt as it was compiled assuming that there was no electricity and no government assistance headed our way.

- Blacksmith
- Brewer/Brewmaster/Moonshiner
- Chef/Cook
- Engineering → Architect, Chemical, Invention, Mechanical
- Farming → Gardener, Farmer, Forager, Herbalist
- Farrier
- Firearm Instructor
- Fireman
- Gatherer → Angler, Hunter (rifle/bow), Trapper
- Leadership/Law → Lawyer, Judge, LEO, Military
- Mechanic
- Medical → Doctor, EMT, Midwife, Nurse
- Trades → Carpentry, Electrical, Landscaping, Masonry, Plumbing, Woodworker

We hope you have enjoyed learning more about what *Preparing to Prepare* means and can take some of this knowledge forward to begin your own preparedness journey. Not just for you, but for your family and extended family, friends, group, or community regardless of the duration you identified.

Please consider leaving a review on Amazon.

Feel free to reach out to the publisher directly with any specific inquiries regarding the content, embedded links, noted resources, or to simply ask a follow-up question at djkpublishinghouse@gmail.com.

To follow the author and see what he is up to as he continues his own preparedness journey or in his writing, please visit his website at https://www.davidjkershner.com.

Index

Recommended Reading & Noted Websites

Adamant, A. (2018, November 9). *Woodlot - 16 Medicinal Trees for Your Herbal Medicine Chest*. Retrieved from Practical Self Reliance: https://practicalselfreliance.com/medicinal-trees/

Aman, D. (2011). *Fire Skills - 50 Methods for Starting Fires Without Matches*. CreateSpace Independent Publishing Platform.

Army, D. o. (2019). *The Official U.S. Army Illustrated Guide to Edible Wild Plants*. Lyons Press; Illustrated edition.

Backer, MD, MPH, H. D., Derlet, MD, R. W., & Hill, PhD, V. R. (2019, October 23). *Water - Wilderness Medical Society Clinical Practice Guidelines for Water Disinfection for Wilderness, International Travel, and Austere Situations*. Retrieved from Wilderness and Environmental Medicine: https://www.wemjournal.org/article/S1080-6032(19)30116-4/fulltext

Bartholomew, M., & Foundation, S. F. (2018). *All New Square Foot Gardening, 3rd Edition, Fully Updated: MORE Projects - NEW Solutions - GROW Vegetables Anywhere (All New Square Foot Gardening, 9)*. Cool Springs Press; 3rd edition.

Beard, D. C. (2012). *Shelters, Shacks, and Shanties: A Guide to Building Shelters in the Wilderness*. Empire Books.

Bryce, J. (2020). *CONTAINER GARDENING FOR BEGINNERS: : Essential Beginner's Guide to Organic Gardening: Growing Vegetables, Fruits, Herbs, Edible Flowers, and Ornamental Plants in Pots, Tubs and Other Containers*. Independently published.

Bubel, M., & Bubel, N. (1991). *Root Cellaring: Natural Cold Storage of Fruits & Vegetables*. Storey Publishing, LLC; 2nd edition.

Burch, M. (2014). *The Grow Your Own Food Handbook: A Back to Basics Guide to Planting, Growing, and Harvesting Fruits and Vegetables (Handbook Series)*. Skyhorse; Illustrated edition.

Burns, D., & Burns, S. (2020). *Backyard Beekeeping: Everything You Need to Know to Start Your First Hive*. Rockridge Press; Illustrated edition.

Carlson, J. (2018, September 20). *Woodstoves - 5 Favorites: Wood Burning Cookstoves for the Kitchen*. Retrieved from Remodelista: https://www.remodelista.com/posts/5-favorites-wood-cook-stoves/

Charcoal - 9 Easy Steps to Make Your Own Charcoal. (n.d.). Retrieved from Urban Survival Site: https://urbansurvivalsite.com/9-easy-steps-make-charcoal/

Charcoal - Ultimate Charcoal Guide: Learn How Charcoal is Made and What's Really in Your Fuel. (2020, April 4). Retrieved from Smoked BBQ Source: https://www.smokedbbqsource.com/how-to-make-charcoal/

Courts, D. (2013, October 2). *Charcoal - Make Your Own Charcoal*. Retrieved from Wonder How To - Survival Training: https://survivial-training.wonderhowto.com/how-to/make-your-own-charcoal-0148846/

Daniels, G. (2014). *Container Gardening Month by Month: A Monthly Listing of Tips and Ideas for Creating a Professional Container Garden (The Weekend Gardener Book 1)*.

Dickson, M. (2018). *Where There Is No Dentist*. Hesperian Health Guides; 15th updated printing 2018.

Doyle, G. S. (2010). *When There Is No Doctor: Preventive and Emergency Healthcare in Challenging Times*. Process; Illustrated edition.

Eastman, W. F. (2002). *A Guide to Canning, Freezing, Curing & Smoking Meat, Fish & Game*. Storey Publishing, LLC; Revised and Updated ed. edition.

Elias, T., & Dykeman, P. (2009). *Edible Wild Plants: A North American Field Guide to Over 200 Natural Foods*. Sterling; Illustrated edition.

Ellis, C. (2015). *Prepper's Natural Medicine: Life-Saving Herbs, Essential Oils and Natural Remedies for When There is No Doctor*. Ulysses Press; 1st edition.

Espiritu, K. (2019). *Field Guide to Urban Gardening: How to Grow Plants, No Matter Where You Live: Raised Beds, Vertical Gardening, Indoor Edibles, Balconies and Rooftops, Hydroponics*. Cool Springs Press; Illustrated edition.

Firearms - Apply for a License (FFL). (n.d.). Retrieved from ATF.gov: https://www.atf.gov/firearms/apply-license

Firearms - FFL License Cost [2020] - How Much is a Federal Firearm License? (2020, January 4). Retrieved from Rocket FFL: https://www.atf.gov/firearms/apply-license

Firearms - Front Sight Courses. (n.d.). Retrieved from Front Sight Firearms Training Institute: https://www.frontsight.com/Courses.asp

Firearms - Gun Laws: Guide to the Interstate Transportation of Firearms. (n.d.). Retrieved from NRA-ILA: https://www.nraila.org/gun-laws/

Firearms - New York City Demonstrates the Danger to Freedom and Safety of Firearm Licensing Laws. (2021, January 4). Retrieved from NRA-ILA: https://www.nraila.org/articles/20210104/new-york-city-demonstrates-the-danger-to-freedom-and-safety-of-firearm-licensing-laws

Firearms - Training Location Search. (n.d.). Retrieved from Project Appleseed: https://appleseedinfo.org/

Firearms - Valor Ridge Courses. (n.d.). Retrieved from Valor Ridge: https://www.valorridge.com/pages/classes

FMA. (2016, September 9). *The Noodles that Cause Chronic Inflammation, Weight Gain, Alzheimer's and Parkinson's disease*. Retrieved from HealthyCures: http://healthycures.org/noodles-cause-chronic-inflammation-weight-gain-alzheimers-parkinsons-disease

Foster, S., & Duke, J. A. (2014). *Peterson Field Guide to Medicinal Plants and Herbs of Eastern and Central North America, Third Edition*. Houghton Mifflin Harcourt; Third edition.

Gardening - 23 Types of Berry Bushes. (n.d.). Retrieved from Leafy Place: https://leafyplace.com/types-of-berries/

Gardening - Cold Hardiness Zone. (n.d.). Retrieved from USDA Agricultural Research Service: https://planthardiness.ars.usda.gov/PHZMWeb/Default.aspx

Gardening - Extend the Growing Season. (n.d.). Retrieved from Safer Brand: https://www.saferbrand.com/articles/extend-growing-season

Gardening - Growing Guide. (n.d.). Retrieved from Stark Bros: https://www.starkbros.com/growing-guide

Gardening - Orchard (Fruit). (n.d.). Retrieved from Stark Bros: https://www.starkbros.com/growing-guide/article/adding-fruit-to-your-homestead

Gardening - Plant Suppliers. (n.d.). Retrieved from Start Bros: https://www.starkbros.com

Gardening - Planting Raspberries Guide. (2020, August 28). Retrieved from Happy DIY Home: https://happydiyhome.com/planting-raspberries/

Gardening - Soil Sample Testing Sites. (n.d.). Retrieved from State-by-State List of Soil Testing Labs: https://gardeningproductsreview.com/state-by-state-list-soil-testing-labs-cooperative-extension-offices/

Geologic Survey - National Geologic Map Database. (n.d.). Retrieved from USGS.gov: https://ngmdb.usgs.gov/ngm-bin/ngm_compsearch.pl

HAM Radio - Courses and Training. (n.d.). Retrieved from National Association of Amateur Radio: http://www.arrl.org/courses-training

HAM Radio - Find an Amateur Radio License Class. (n.d.). Retrieved from National Association of Amateur Radio: http://www.arrl.org/find-an-amateur-radio-license-class

HAM Radio - HAM Radio Licenses. (n.d.). Retrieved from National Association of Amateur Radio: http://www.arrl.org/ham-radio-licenses

Hill, L., & Perry, L. (2011). *The Fruit Gardener's Bible: A Complete Guide to Growing Fruits and Nuts in the Home Garden*. Storey Publishing, LLC; Illustrated edition.

Hobson, P. (1983). *Build Your Own Underground Root Cellar*. Storey Publishing, LLC; Illustrated edition.

Hume, D. (2018). *Fire Making: The Forgotten Art of Conjuring Flame with Spark, Tinder, and Skill*. The Experiment; Illustrated edition.

Israel, D. L. (1995, February/March). *Woodlot - Small Woodlot Management*. Retrieved from Mother Earth News: https://www.motherearthnews.com/homesteading-and-livestock/woodlot-management-zmaz95fmztak

Kaller, B. (2018, August 14). *Charcoal - Making Charcoal*. Retrieved from Resilience.org: https://www.resilience.org/stories/2018-08-14/making-charcoal/

Kershner, D. J. (2020). *Home Remedies, Poultices, Salves & Tinctures*. DJK Publishing House.

Kochanski, M. (2012). *21 Native Wild Edible Plants*. Karamat Wilderness Ways.

Kochanski, M. (2013). *The Lean To and Its Variants Used in Survival and Bush Bough Beds*. Karamat Wilderness Ways.

LaLiberte, K. (n.d.). *Gardening - Season Extending Techniques*. Retrieved from Gardeners Supply Company: https://www.gardeners.com/how-to/season-extending-techniques/5063.html

MacWelch, T. (2019, October 16). *Shelters - Survival Shelters: 15 Best Designs and How to Build Them*. Retrieved from Outdoor Life: https://www.outdoorlife.com/survival-shelters-15-best-designs-wilderness-shelters/

Madigan, C. (2009). *The Backyard Homestead: Produce all the food you need on just a quarter acre!* Storey Publishing.

Marianski, A., Marianski, R., & Marianski, S. (2012). *Meat Smoking and Smokehouse Design*. Bookmagic LLC; 3rd ed. edition.

Markham, B. L. (2010). *Mini Farming: Self Sufficiency on a 1/4 Acre*. Skyhorse; Illustrated edition.

Maxwell, S., MacKenzie, J., & (Illustrator), L. C. (2010). *The Complete Root Cellar Book: Building Plans, Uses and 100 Recipes*. Robert Rose; Illustrated edition.

McDonald, M. (2019, September 2). *Charcoal - How to Make Your Own Charcoal*. Retrieved from Popular Mechanics: https://www.popularmechanics.com/home/outdoor-projects/a28848441/how-to-make-charcoal/

Medical - Class Programs. (n.d.). Retrieved from American Red Cross: https://www.redcross.org/take-a-class

Medical - Online CPR Training Videos. (n.d.). Retrieved from ProCPR by ProTrainings: https://www.procpr.org/training

Medical - Training Programs. (n.d.). Retrieved from American Safety & Health Institute: https://emergencycare.hsi.com/cpr-and-first-aid-courses

MissouriVillian. (n.d.). *Fire - 7 Methods of Primitive Fire Starting*. Retrieved from https://www.instructables.com/id/7-Methods-of-Primitive-Fire-Starting/

Noonan, T. (2020, January 3). *Puerto Rico: This Is What Living in a 6 Month-Blackout Looks Like*. Retrieved from Ask a Prepper: https://www.askaprepper.com/puerto-rico-this-is-what-living-in-a-6-month-blackout-looks-like

Nyerges, C., & Cornell, A. (2020). *Guide to Making Fire without Matches: Tips, Tactics, and Techniques for Starting a Fire in Any Situation.* Skyhorse.

Oliver, E. W. (2020). *HOW TO BUILD A SMOKEHOUSE: A Beginner's To Pro Guide on How to Build A Smokehouse From Scratch To Finish On A Budget.* Independently published.

Orienteering - Club Search. (n.d.). Retrieved from Orienteering USA: https://orienteeringusa.org/events/clubs/

Orienteering - Orienteering Basics: How to Get Started. (n.d.). Retrieved from REI: https://www.rei.com/learn/expert-advice/orienteering-basics.html

Paris, J. (2019). *HUGELKULTUR - Raised Bed Vegetable Gardening With Hugelkultur; An Introduction To Growing Vegetables In Tree Cuttings And Turf Heaps (Vegetable Gardening Shorts).* Independently published.

Phillips, M. (2012). *The Holistic Orchard: Tree Fruits and Berries the Biological Way.* Chelsea Green Publishing; Illustrated edition.

Pina, L. (1984, March/April). *Add a Hand Pump to an Electric Well.* Retrieved from Mother Earth News: https://www.motherearthnews.com/diy/hand-pump-electric-well-zmaz84zloeck

Plocher, T., & Parke, B. (2008). *Northern Winework: Growing Grapes and Making Wine in Cold Climates (2nd Edition).* Eau Claire Printing; Second Edition.

Portability - How I Built My 25 Pound Bug Out Bag. (n.d.). Retrieved from Graywolf Survival: http://graywolfsurvival.com/66545/how-to-build-ultimate-25-pound-bug-bag/

Powers, T. (2012). *The Organic Backyard Vineyard: A Step-by-Step Guide to Growing Your Own Grapes.* Timber Press.

Precious Metals - Consumer Column: Ten Tips for Selling Grandma's Silverware. (2013, December 27). Retrieved from Fort Worth Star Telegram: https://www.star-telegram.com/news/business/article3840991.html

Precious Metals - Dealer. (n.d.). Retrieved from JM Bullion: https://www.jmbullion.com/

Precious Metals - Dealer. (n.d.). Retrieved from APMEX: https://www.apmex.com/

Precious Metals - Dealer. (n.d.). Retrieved from Provident Metals: https://www.providentmetals.com/

Reloading - Best Reloading Presses for Beginners. (2019, January 17). Retrieved from Pew Pew Tactical: https://www.pewpewtactical.com/best-reloading-presses-beginners/

Reloading - Reloading Press Products. (n.d.). Retrieved from Lee Precision Inc.: https://leeprecision.com/reloading-presses/

Reloading - Reloading Press Products. (n.d.). Retrieved from RCBS Precisioneered Reloading: https://www.rcbs.com/

Reloading - Reloading Press Products. (n.d.). Retrieved from Hornady: https://www.hornady.com/reloading/presses/

Sharan, G. (2011, Spring). *Harvesting Dew with Radiation Cooled Condensers to Supplement Drinking Water Supply in Semi-arid Coastal Northwest India*. Retrieved from Semantic Scholar: https://pdfs.semanticscholar.org/b82a/af77fca4b6ebf78923a86c82be4ff1a2c e24.pdf

Shelters - Long Term Survival Shelters from Alone. (n.d.). Retrieved from Survival Skills Guide: https://survivalskills.guide/long-term-survival-shelters-alone/

Smith, E. C. (2011). *The Vegetable Gardener's Container Bible: How to Grow a Bounty of Food in Pots, Tubs, and Other Containers*. Storey Publishing, LLC; Illustrated edition.

Smokehouse - How-To Build a Smokehouse (Part 1 - Foundation). (2015, May 2). Retrieved from YouTube - Tim Farmer Channel: https://www.youtube.com/watch?v=UjsqfSbK1ro

Smokehouse - How-To Build a Smokehouse (Part 2 - Flue Pipe and Building Blocks). (2015, May 16). Retrieved from YouTube - Tim Farmer Channel: https://www.youtube.com/watch?v=zaVcTYfWBGQ

Smokehouse - How-To Build a Smokehouse (Part 3 - Fire Box). (2015, May 23). Retrieved from YouTube - Tim Farmer Channel: https://www.youtube.com/watch?v=ySi1HEeUN6Q

Smokehouse - How-To Build a Smokehouse (Part 4 - Roof and Wood Frame). (2015, May 30). Retrieved from YouTube - Tim Farmer Channel: https://www.youtube.com/watch?v=2rNRxTekOV8

Smokehouse - How-To Build a Smokehouse (Part 5 - Final Steps). (2015, June 13). Retrieved from YouTube - Tim Farmer Channel: https://www.youtube.com/watch?v=vZpD3FKwn4s

Solar - Deep Cycle Batteries. (n.d.). Retrieved from Real Goods: https://realgoods.com/off-grid-solar/deep-cycle-batteries

Solar - Enphase. (n.d.). Retrieved from Enphase: https://enphase.com/en-us/ensemble-technology-enphase-installers

Solar - Tesla Powerwall. (n.d.). Retrieved from Tesla: https://www.tesla.com/powerwall

Solar - Water Pumps. (n.d.). Retrieved from RPS Solar Pumps: https://www.rpssolarpumps.com/

Thayer, S. (2006). *The Forager's Harvest: A Guide to Identifying, Harvesting, and Preparing Edible Wild Plants*. Foragers Harvest Press; 1st edition.

Topographic Maps - Free Printable USGS PDF Quads. (n.d.). Retrieved from National Geographic: https://www.natgeomaps.com/trail-maps/pdf-quads

Vivante, T. G., (Foreward), D. M., & (Foreward), E. C. (2007). *Preserving Food without Freezing or Canning: Traditional Techniques Using Salt, Oil, Sugar, Alcohol, Vinegar, Drying, Cold Storage, and Lactic Fermentation*. Chelsea Green Publishing; New edition.

Water - Air Well/Condenser. (n.d.). Retrieved from Wikipedia:
https://en.wikipedia.org/wiki/Air_well_(condenser)

Water - Air Well/Condesnser. (n.d.). Retrieved from Permies.com:
https://permies.com/t/airwell

Water - Disinfection Search Results. (n.d.). Retrieved from Wilderness and
Environmental Medicine:
https://www.wemjournal.org/action/doSearch?text1=water+disinfection&field1=AllField

Water - Hand Pump. (n.d.). Retrieved from Wikipedia:
https://en.wikipedia.org/wiki/Hand_pump

Water - Hand Pump - Deep Well Hand Pump Install. (2017, February 13). Retrieved
from YouTube - Through Our Eyes Channel:
https://www.youtube.com/watch?v=It3CvoRxmmE

Water - Hand Pump - Hand Pump Install. (2015, July 17). Retrieved from YouTube
- Prepper Recon Channel:
https://www.youtube.com/watch?v=GlRAm5gaUhg

Water - Well Water - Running a Well Pump off a Generator. (2015, May 7).
Retrieved from YouTube - Yanasa TV Channel:
https://www.youtube.com/watch?v=tLNZMY16044

Water - Well Water - Running a Well Pump off Batteries Part 1. (2019, February 6).
Retrieved from YouTube - Jay Summet Channel:
https://www.youtube.com/watch?v=J1rrgxM9Nn8

Water - Well Water - Running a Well Pump off Batteries Part 2. (2019, February 12).
Retrieved from YouTube - Jay Summet Channel:
https://www.youtube.com/watch?v=7nsMR9TmUXY

Water - Wind Pump. (n.d.). Retrieved from Wikipedia:
https://en.wikipedia.org/wiki/Windpump

Water - Wind Pump - Backyard Wind Water Pump. (2009, April 24). Retrieved from
YouTube - Kirsten Dirksen Channel:
https://www.youtube.com/watch?v=cnY2ejP43bA

Water - Wind Pump - Off Grid Water System. (2017, July 22). Retrieved from
YouTube - Simple Little Life Channel:
https://www.youtube.com/watch?v=8T-6CAsvDgQ

Water Filtration - Alexapure. (n.d.). Retrieved from My Patriot Supply:
https://www.mypatriotsupply.com/water_filtration_s/181.htm

Water Filtration - Big Berkey. (n.d.). Retrieved from Berkey:
https://www.berkeywater.com/big-berkey-system-2-25-gal/

Water Harvesting - Rainwater H20G. (n.d.). Retrieved from Rainwater Hog:
http://www.rainwaterhog.com/

Water Harvesting - Rainwater Harvesting Cisterns and Tanks. (n.d.). Retrieved from
Innovative Water Solutions:
https://www.watercache.com/portfolio/rainwater-cisterns-tanks

Water Harvesting - waterBOB. (n.d.). Retrieved from waterBOB:
https://www.waterbob.com

Weeks, D. (2012, April 13). *Woodlot - Managing Your Woodlot.* Retrieved from
Successful Farming: https://www.agriculture.com/family/living-the-
country-life/managing-your-woodlot

Weir, B. (2017, December 21). *Hellish summer of hurricanes smashes FEMA.*
Retrieved from CNN: http://www.cnn.com/2017/12/19/politics/summer-of-
hurricanes-broke-fema-weir/index.html

Werner, D., Thuman, C., & Maxwell, J. (2017). *Where There Is No Doctor: A
Village Health Care Handbook.* Hesperian Health Guides; Revised edition.

Whitbread, D. (2021, January 2). *Top 10 Food Highest in Vitamin C.* Retrieved from
My Food Data: https://www.myfooddata.com/articles/vitamin-c-foods.php

Woodlot - Managing Your Woodlot: Harvesting and Renewing It. (2010, November
11). Retrieved from YouTube - PublicResourceOrg Channel:
https://www.youtube.com/watch?v=Dd1PwIoH7dg

Woodstoves - 10 Tips for Choosing the Perfect Wood Cookstove. (n.d.). Retrieved
from Joybilee Farm: https://joybileefarm.com/perfect-wood-cook-stove/

Woodstoves - My Kingdom for a Cookstove. (2017, October 11). Retrieved from 5
Dog Farm: https://www.5dog.farm/my-kingdom-for-a-cookstove/

Woodstoves - Products. (n.d.). Retrieved from Obadiah's Woodstoves:
https://www.discountstoves.net/wood-cook-stoves-s/37.htm

Woodstoves - Products. (n.d.). Retrieved from WoodCookStove.com:
https://www.woodcookstove.com/wood-burning-cook-stoves.html

Also by David J. Kershner
www.davidjkershner.com

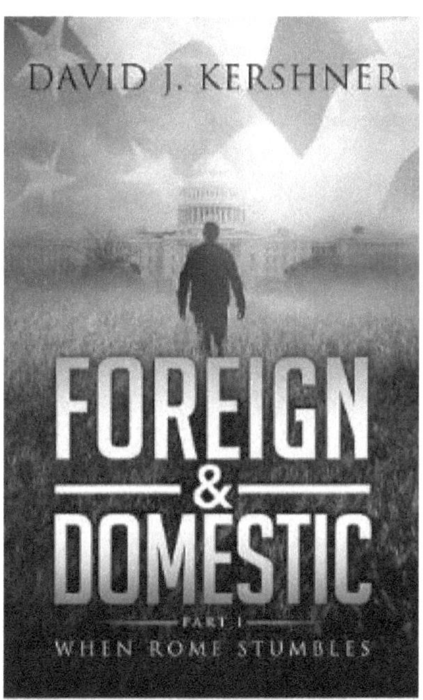

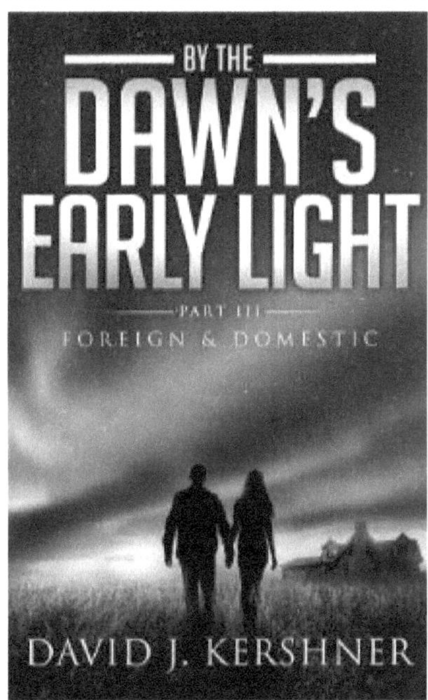

COLDER
WEATHER
PART IV
FOREIGN & DOMESTIC
DAVID J. KERSHNER

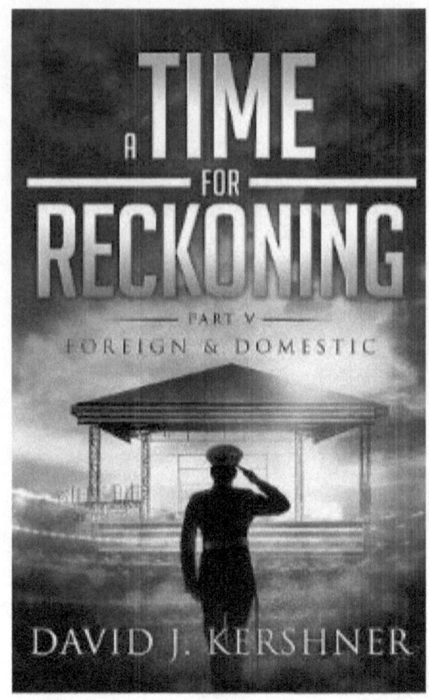

A TIME
FOR
RECKONING
PART V
FOREIGN & DOMESTIC
DAVID J. KERSHNER

JUST A SMALL
GATHERING,
VOLUME I
A Guide to Entertaining Small Groups of Family & Friends
By:
David Kershner & Scott Boles